CAREERMAP

*Deciding What You Want
Getting It
and Keeping It!*

Dr. Neil M. Yeager

Illustrations by David Gordon

WILEY

JOHN WILEY & SONS, INC.
New York • Chichester • Brisbane • Toronto • Singapore

Publisher: Stephen Kippur
Editor: Katherine Schowalter
Managing Editor: Andrew Hoffer
Editing, Design, and Production: G&H SOHO, Ltd.

All the stories presented in this book are based on real experience. Except where specific permission was granted, the names and details of the stories were changed to protect the privacy of people who prefer to not be identified as career changers. In some cases, a composite view of several individuals was presented to illustrate a point.

This publication is designed to provide accurate and authoritative information in regard to the subject matter covered. It is sold with the understanding that the publisher is not engaged in rendering legal, accounting, or other professional service. If legal advice or other expert assistance is required, the services of a competent professional person should be sought. FROM A DECLARATION OF PRINCIPLES JOINTLY ADOPTED BY A COMMITTEE OF THE AMERICAN BAR ASSOCIATION AND A COMMITTEE OF PUBLISHERS.

Library of Congress Cataloging-in-Publication Data

Yeager, Neil M.
  CareerMap: deciding what you want, getting it, and keeping it!

    1. Vocational guidance. 2. Career development.
I. Title. II. Title: CareerMap.
HF5381.Y43 1988   650.1   88-17172
ISBN 0-471-61015-1
ISBN 0-471-61014-3 (pbk.)

Printed in the United States of America

89 10 9 8 7 6 5 4

To Cletha and Ben,
whose love and support inspire my work

ACKNOWLEDGMENTS

I would like to thank my clients, who have taught me much of what I know about career change. I would also like to thank my wife, Cletha Roney, who read, listened, gave me ideas, and put up with me; Miriam Williford, who encouraged and supported me and gave me some really good stories; my editor at John Wiley, Katherine Schowalter, for her good eye, good judgment, and candor; David King for his careful editing; and my agent Elizabeth Frost Knappman for her perseverance and enthusiasm.

I would like to thank my friends and colleagues at the University of Massachusetts at Amherst for their help and support: Judy Wardlaw for her careful reading and careful thoughts; David Gordon for his great illustrations; Debbie Lyon, Anne Jenkins, and Laura Howard for their technical expertise; and Don Carew, Ed Travis, Diane Flaherty, Donna Mellen, Sher Hruska, Mike Manley, and Mary Young for their support, confidence, and enthusiasm.

PREFACE

If you were born between 1935 and 1970, you live in a world far different from those born before you. If you plan to work into the next century, you will have a career far more turbulent than those of your predecessors.

The advent of the information age, the globalization of the world economy, and the limitations of both natural and human-engineered resources dictate the change. The most dramatic shift, and the impetus for this book, is that throughout your career, you need to decide what you want and what you have to offer. You then need to embark on a deliberate strategy for getting work that satisfies you and uses your most valuable assets. Finally, you need to strengthen your position to ensure that you keep what you have gained.

You will change careers an unpredictable number of times. You will probably not stay long enough in any organization to earn the proverbial gold watch.

This is not a disaster; it is a blessing. How many of you could imagine staying in your current job or organization for the rest of your life? For many, such a possibility is inconceivable. Today, most people's careers are more like the expanding universe than the rock-solid earth. This notion of the ever-expanding nature of your career is the driving force behind this book.

As the result of a process developed and refined over the past seven years in workshops I have conducted on career management, I have designed a proven system for managing your career. That system, presented in this book, will help you determine what you want, share with you specific strategies for getting it, and show you what to do to keep it. This systematic, user-friendly method will help you to identify what aspects of yourself to market, how to market them, and what to do to maintain your high market value. It is a system that I've seen work for many people and it *can* work for you.

Most important in approaching the process in this book is understanding and accepting the inevitability of change—in your own priorities, in the job market, and in the organizations for which you work. Your career success will be determined by your ability to predict, manage, and adapt to these changes.

The world is much more complicated than it used to be. The challenges are great, but so are the opportunities. The volatile marketplace we so quaintly refer to as "the world of work" can offer a thrilling journey full of opportunity or it can be a frightening maze full of traps. Why not choose opportunity over entrapment? I hope you do so, and I wish you luck in your efforts.

Neil Yeager
Amherst, MA

CONTENTS

Introduction   1

PART 1:   TAKING STOCK   5

Chapter 1   Taking Control   7
             The Power of Belief / Reframe Exercise

Chapter 2   Assessing Your Personal Potential   15
             From Novice to Expert / The CareerMap Profile /
             Options... A Blessing and a Curse / Personal Pri-
             orities / Preferred Work Style / Exploring Inter-
             ests / Competencies / Significant Events Review
             / Knowledge Scan / Skills Review / Preferred
             Workplace Culture / Career Visualization—More
             Than Coincidence / Your CareerMap Profile

Chapter 3   Developing Your Options/
             Making Tough Choices   57
             Having It All / The Awful Truth / Generating Op-
             tions: Forming a CORE Group / Sorting Your Op-
             tions

PART 2:   TAKING OFF   71

Chapter 4   Clearing the Runway:
             Overcoming Obstacles to Change   73
             A Dozen Deadly Demons and the Twelve
             Disciples of Change / Lack of Opportunity / Old
             Dogs / Blowing Your Horn / Politics / Serendipity
             Is No Accident / Change / Where to Start / The
             Universal "They" / Time / Fear of the Unknown /
             Inertia, Laziness, and the Formless Fears / Want-
             ing to Change

Chapter 5   Gaining Altitude: Taking Smart Risks   97
             The Nature of Career Risk Taking / Risk for the
             Sake of Risk / Mastering Risk: A Tale of Two Risk

Takers / Becoming a Renaissance Risk Taker /
The Risk Assessment Process / The Structured
and Fluid Nature of Risk Taking

Chapter 6   *Navigating Your Course: The POINT Process*   115
"P": Persuasive Paper Work
Résumés / Résumés and Personal Style: A Word
Before You Get Started / The Ancient Art of Let-
ter Writing / Cover Letters / Letters of Approach/
Letters and Gatekeepers / A Note on Thank-You
Letters
"O": Occupational Investigation
The Compelling Job Market / Conquering the
Compelling Market Through the Senses
"I": Influential Interviewing
Ten Tips for a Better Job Interview: The Science
of Interviewing / The Art of Interviewing / Style:
More Than Just Clothes and Manners / Being
Your Most Appropriate Self
"N": Networking
Formal Angles /Informal Angles
"T": Tracking Leads
Setting Yourself Apart / Tracking Leads Through
Effective Patterning / Don't Start from Scratch /
Finding Models for Tracking / Tracking Model
Profile

PART 3   TAKING HOLD   167

Chapter 7   *Signing Up*   169
A Good Match Is Hard to Find / Examining the
New Turf / Casing the Culture / Six Sources of
Cultural Information / Examining the Health and
Stability of the Organization / The Zero Advance-
ment Principle (ZAP): How to Avoid Getting
ZAPped / Creating Your Own Career Path / Cut-
ting a Deal: Negotiating for What You Want / The
Six Myths of Salary Negotiation (and the Reali-
ties)

Chapter 8   *Building a Base*   189
The Only Real Security / Mentoring in an Uncertain World / Performance Mentoring Activities / Coaching / Stretching / Modeling / Nondirective Helping / Personal Mentoring Activities / Promoting / Showcasing / Advocating / Inspiring / Friendship / Cross-Gender Mentoring Relationships / Multiple Mentoring Relationships: The Mentoring Mandala

Chapter 9   *Staying on Top*   223
Managing Your Career: "The Boss" Style / Skill Mastery: The Keystone of Your Success / Developing Mastery / The Seven Sides of Every Organization / Politics / Power / The Six Sources of Personal Power / Structure / Patterns of Organizational Communication / History / Agenda / Image / Mergers, Buyouts, Acquisitions, and Your Career

Epilogue   257
Index   259

INTRODUCTION

You are about to work with a book that can forever change the way you view your career. If you're like most Americans, when you think about your career, you think about your job, your organization, or your current profession. This book will shift that focus back to where it belongs: to yourself. And you will learn how to play an active role in making that shift.

I wrote this book to inform, inspire, and involve the reader. Whenever possible, I've included stories of people who have struggled with, and taken charge of, their careers. I believe these stories can motivate you much more effectively than the most powerful speech ever could.

To get the most out of this book, you need to commit yourself to working with me as I guide you through a process that has worked for many other people over the past seven years. You will be asked to make many decisions along the way. Some will be difficult, but all are essential to gaining and maintaining control over your career.

Knowing where to start and what to do next can be confusing, which is why I created CareerMap. Through this book, I will help you chart your own course by equipping you for your journey and providing guideposts along the way. I believe that if you use CareerMap carefully, as you would a navigational map for a difficult journey, you will reach your destination more quickly, more easily, and with far more energy once you arrive.

You will find that this book is organized to maximize its usefulness as both a book to read from cover to cover and a reference for managing particular career issues. If you need to determine your next career move, launch a job search campaign, and establish yourself in a new position, I suggest that you start at the beginning and move through the entire process. If you know what you want but haven't yet attained it, start with Part 2. If you like the situation you're in but want

to enhance your career and increase your potential, read
Chapters 8 and 9 first; then review Chapters 1, 4, and 5.

Taking Stock: Part 1

Taking stock, the first step, involves identifying your priorities, your personal style, strengths, interests, and fantasies
and gaining a better understanding of the skills and knowledge you bring to any work situation. Once you have clarified your desires and abilities, you will identify the range of
possibilities available and narrow and target your options.

Taking Off: Part 2

Knowing what you want does little good if you don't know
how to get it. Once you've clarified your priorities and what
you have to offer, you will focus on how to achieve your
goals. You will develop and refine all the skills necessary for
establishing yourself in a new career or for enhancing your
role in your current career. You will identify and remove obstacles to change. You will learn a risk-assessment process
that will help you maximize positive results and keep you
from losing your shirt. Finally, you will fine-tune your job
search strategies through the POINT Process (Persuasive
paper work, Occupational investigation, Influential interviewing, Networking, Tracking leads).

Taking Hold: Part 3

Once you understand what you want and how to get it, you
will concentrate on developing key strategies for securing
and keeping what you've sought and attained. By sharpening your negotiation skills, building a base of support, and
refining your understanding of organizational dynamics, you
will create conditions that assure you will stay on top.

Taking and maintaining control of your career takes skill, determination, and courage. You can do it if you are willing to say yes to yourself and no to all the forces that would prefer you not be in charge. Remember, your career is your own. Choose to take control of it, and your life may never be the same.

PART 1
TAKING STOCK

ONE

Taking Control

"WE'RE BORED AS HELL AND WE'RE
NOT GONNA TAKE IT ANYMORE!"

THIS BOOK is about taking control of your career, which sounds easier than it is. If you're like most people, you feel less than powerful in managing your career. If you've ever sat at home waiting for the phone to ring, if you've ever come in second for that perfect position, if you've ever watched a colleague or, worse, an outsider take a position that you were entitled to, you surely know what I mean. The fact is:

**Career management is simple,
but it is not easy.**

The mechanics are straightforward; simply follow the guidelines given in this book. The hard part is:

**To really manage your career,
you must believe in your ability to do so.**

Many beliefs can contribute to your sense of powerlessness over your own career. A few of the more deadly ones are:

- To really move, you need connections, and I don't have any.
- I don't have the right degree, qualifications, training, and so on.
- There are no positions available.
- The competition is overwhelming.
- I don't know anything about that type of organization.

Such beliefs prevent an empowered approach to career management. The first step in moving from being powerless to empowered is to change those beliefs. This change, which psychologists call a *positive reframe*, involves shifting your

8

beliefs from negative to positive. For example, here are the beliefs listed above reframed in positive terms:

- Everyone has connections; I just have to figure out what mine are and use them effectively.
- I have skills and abilities to offer any employer in need of a bright, committed worker; I just need to figure out how to present them effectively.
- I only need one job (for now). Paying attention to statistics will only discourage me. Besides, if they really want me, they'll find a place for me.
- I need to present myself in the best light possible to beat the competition.
- People are people. If I learn to read organizational cultures well, I can see through the differences and contribute in my own way.

You may hold some of the negative beliefs I've mentioned, or you may have others. In either case, reframing them in positive terms will improve your attitude and increase your motivation to manage your career.

The Power of Belief

There are many vivid examples in our culture of people who have reframed their beliefs and as a result have done astounding things with their lives. Ted Kennedy, Jr., lost his leg to cancer. But rather than accept his fate as handicapped, he developed an entire movement of "physically challenged" athletes and has achieved tremendous results as a skier and runner. He has also harnessed the power of belief and directed his energies toward motivating others. We've all seen remarkable film clips of people playing guitar, typing, or painting with their feet. The most vivid example I've seen is an armless woman who, determined to live a normal life, independently nursed and raised her child. Where would these people be if they believed they were as helpless as others think they are?

People with dyslexia are a less obvious group of positive reframers. The list of great achievers who were dyslexic is long; Albert Einstein, Thomas Edison, Woodrow Wilson, and William Butler Yeats are but a few. Imagine how far these people would have gone if they had accepted their tendency to see words backwards as a limitation rather than a challenge.

One common characteristic of all these people is that rather than be controlled by forces, even powerful ones, affecting their lives, they chose to summon their own resources, harness their energies, and take control.

Reframe Exercise

To take control, you need to reframe your negative beliefs in positive terms. Spend a few minutes now thinking about times when you feel discouraged about your career. Think about your job duties, relationships at work, potential for future growth, and the like.

Write down five statements that summarize some of your negative feelings about your career (refer back to the examples if you get stuck).

Negative Beliefs

1. _Opportunities goes to outsiders_
2. _Marginalization prohibits contribution_
3. _Organizationally buried_
4. _____
5. _____

Now, think about what you might do to change each belief so that it reflects a positive view. At this point, it's important to realize that some shifts in belief may also require a shift in behavior.

For example: *My job is terribly boring.*

This negative belief can be particularly debilitating, but to simply say "my job is very exciting" would only be to fool yourself. In this case, the positive reframe requires a change in behavior as well as a shift in attitude.

For example: *I'm going to figure out a way to make my job more interesting and talk it over with my boss.*

Although it is more complicated than a simple reframe, a shift in attitude *and* behavior will have the same effect: giving you a greater sense of control over your situation.

Now, take your five negative beliefs and reframe them in positive terms in the space provided. When necessary, include the acts you need to perform in order to achieve a realistic reframe.

Positive Reframes

1. _____
2. _____
3. _____
4. _____
5. _____

Now that you've completed this first transition, you're on your way to taking control of your career. This does not mean that you will pretend there are no external forces affecting your career. Rather, it means that you will accept external forces, knowing that because you are well prepared, you can handle whatever comes.

Over the past seven years, I have worked with many career changers from all walks of life and at all organizational levels. Many have been successful at harnessing and managing their careers; others have been less so. I have spent long hours struggling to understand the difference between those who succeed and those who don't; and after eliminating all the complicated explanations, I have arrived at a simple truth:

**Those who do it, do it;
those who don't, don't.**

It *is* as simple as that. Those who succeed in managing their careers to their own satisfaction are willing to take risks (albeit careful ones), are willing to make their desires known, and have thick-enough skins to tolerate rejection.

**The road to success is
paved with rejection letters.**

Getting the job you want is like getting a book published. Ask any best-selling author how many times a first manuscript was rejected before finally getting accepted, and most will tell you it took ten or twenty submissions. We don't know how many rejections the great unpublished books received, but I'll bet most were fewer than ten. The choice is yours:

**Would you rather be a proud loser
or a satisfied winner?**

I recently spoke with a woman who had a successful career as an appraiser for a large real estate firm. After leaving the firm because of a conflict with management, she decided to look for appraisal work at a bank. She had two interviews, and both bankers told her they wanted someone with banking experience. As a result of these two rejections, she decided she was unemployable in banking and reluctantly began to pursue other options.

After speaking with her for several minutes and learning that she did indeed have extensive real estate experience, I suspected her problem was more one of access and persistence than of experience. I suggested that instead of giving up on banking, she might do better if she could get a friend or acquaintance to help her get in the door. I also said she needed to start thinking about the difference between realtors and bankers. Upon hearing these suggestions, she became abrupt. She implied that she could get work on her merits and did not need to play up to or oblige herself to anyone. I tried to persuade her that she need not be insincere or become obligated beyond the point at which a thank-you note would suffice, but she would not listen. I suspect she remains proudly unemployed. Negative beliefs about rejection, the use of contacts, and knowledge of your market can greatly limit your possibilities; positive beliefs about these things can greatly expand your options.

So, if you're ready to take charge of your career and chart your own future, fortify your positive beliefs, move on to Chapter 2, and begin developing your CareerMap Profile.

TWO

Assessing Your Personal Potential

From Novice to Expert

Tom H.: A Case of Misjudged Ability

WHEN TOM H. came to see me in the summer of 1984, he was as dejected as anyone I'd seen in my work as a career consultant. For the past seven years, he had worked in day care, first as a teacher and then as an administrator, and he was convinced that he would never find work outside the field. The first thing I asked him to do was to shift his beliefs about his potential (using the strategy outlined in Chapter 1). His second task was to figure out what, in fact, his potential was.

He began by examining his personal priorities and found, not surprisingly, that they had shifted since he began working in day care. He then looked at his preferred work style and found he was less interested in working with kids than in using his creative abilities. (He played the guitar, but we agreed he did not have commercial potential.)

Next, he looked at his interests and areas of knowledge, which revealed he was fond of, and had dabbled in, computers. In looking at the types of people with whom he preferred to work, he found that he was now drawn to entrepreneurial and intellectual individuals rather than the more familiar social and emotional groups.

When he examined his skills, he found his strengths were organization, design, and problem solving. Finally, he pursued his fantasy of the ideal work situation and found himself imagining a large, resourceful, innovative organization (unlike any day-care center either of us had ever seen).

After helping Tom develop his CareerMap Profile and giving him a little advice, I sent him on his way. The following are excerpts from a letter I received from Tom in January, 1985, six months after I last spoke with him.

> I am currently working at Coleco as an educational product designer; specifically, software design for children 3 years old

to 10 years old. You might recall that I told you that I got the job through someone in my personal network; he heard of the job opening and recommended me for the position. Your advice on networking really paid off.

I have thoroughly enjoyed the job at Coleco. The design process has required the development of original ideas and concepts, writing comprehensive product descriptions, directing teams of software engineers and graphic artists, software integrity testing, and directing all aspects of production to product completion. I've designed for Adam, Atari, Commodore, and Apple. The experience has been very positive. The environment is creative; I feel valued and appropriately well paid.

Of all the things I've learned on this job, the most shocking lesson is in corporate reality and the power of the stock market. You might have seen in the news that Coleco has sold off the Adam computer to a retail chain. The home computer market is very volatile at the moment and probably will be for the next year. Because the computer has been sold off, my department will soon be let go in its entirety. In fact, there have been massive layoffs already. I'm one of the few survivors, but I expect to be going very soon.

I've started my job search and dug out all of the materials from your course. The amazing thing is that this time people are actually calling me! I've had calls from Texas, California, and New York from people I never contacted. I don't know how they got my name. It's a totally new experience. I've also been approached by a number of headhunters looking to work on my behalf (and with the employer footing the bill).

Well, even though the search is very different this time around, it is still not an easy process. I've rewritten my résumé (enclosed) and contacted a number of potential employers and resource people. I would like to stay in educational software design. I enjoy the creative process and feel confident and comfortable with it. Any and all leads would be appreciated.

Even though Coleco has bottomed out on me, I feel positive about the whole experience. I feel I've found a solid direction that combines my previous experience in education with newfound skills in the computer industry. The rewards are great, and the potential for growth is exciting. Please tell your next class that if I can do it, anyone can!

Last I heard, Tom had left Coleco and taken a job with a major publishing house in Boston, where he continues to work in the area of educational software design. What strikes me about Tom's case is that once he shifted his beliefs about what he was capable of doing and clarified his strengths, priorities, interests, and desires, he made what he wanted to occur happen. Another thing about people like Tom—and I've known lots of them—is that they handle adversity extremely well. Once these people become clear about what they have to offer and what they want, they allow their internal resources to prevail over whatever external forces get in their way.

In this next section, you will develop your own CareerMap Profile to help you chart your own future.

The CareerMap Profile

A Seven-Step Process

The method I present here for assessing your own potential was developed, refined, and modified over the course of seven years of conducting career management workshops. There is no magic formula involved, nor will the completion of the CareerMap Profile land you your next job. What it will do is provide you with a concise view of your strengths, priorities, interests, and ideals. By helping you sort out your options, it will give you a clear sense of direction. It will help you determine what you need to do to make your current work more satisfying and your future work more rewarding. Finally, it will provide you with essential information for marketing yourself.

Because you are unique, your requirements for a satisfying career are different from those of anyone else. In seven years of developing CareerMap Profiles, I've never seen two identical ones. This unique picture of who you are will be the basis for your charting your own future and will provide you with an essential frame of reference as you move through the rest of this book.

Options... A Blessing and a Curse

A word before we begin: Throughout the rest of this chapter, you will be asked to make some forced choices. The word *forced* is the key here. More than ever before, we live in a world full of options of all kinds. For example, a friend recently commented on the anxiety she now feels when she walks into an ice-cream store and faces an overwhelming range of choices.

**Having a lot of options
is like having a lot of relatives.
You're glad you have them,
but sometimes you wish
they would go away.**

People who seek to gain control over their careers face a series of choices that must be made in order to proceed. The activities presented in this chapter will challenge your decision-making powers and *force* you to make choices because:

**The only way to do it
is to do it.**

Charlie N.: A Shift in Priorities

Charlie N. was frustrated and confused when he came to see me in the fall of 1986. He had a good job with a major insurance company, had moved up the corporate ladder, and was about to become a senior manager in underwriting. For the past fifteen years, Charlie had refined his skills and expanded his knowledge to the point where he knew as much about his business as anyone else. The goals he had when he started at the age of twenty-one had been achieved. He had security, precision work, a relaxed work environment, and the respect of his peers.

Why was he seeking the advice of a career consultant? Charlie's own words say it best: "I became very depressed when I realized that as long as I didn't drool too much, they would probably let me sit at the same desk, doing the same thing, for the *next* fifteen years."

After a brief discussion, it became clear to both of us that Charlie was going through an experience common to many people in midcareer: a shift in priorities. No longer satisfied with the status quo, Charlie had new priorities; he wanted adventure, challenge, and the opportunity to influence others.

After he completed his CareerMap Profile and did some careful planning, Charlie approached management with his superior record and broad knowledge base and requested a transfer to training and development. He also joined the public speaking group Toastmasters and intends to become the most dynamic underwriting trainer the industry has ever seen.

Charlie's case highlights the benefits to organizations of supporting employees' efforts to manage their own careers. Charlie gained a new opportunity with plenty of the adventure, challenge, and influence he was seeking, and his company gained a renewed employee with increased commitment and motivation to perform at a high level.

Personal Priorities

Each of us looks for certain qualities in our work that make it worthwhile. Some want adventure; others want to help people; others thrive on working under pressure. A critical factor for attaining job satisfaction is the molding of a job to accommodate your top priorities.

The following exercise asks you to consider a range of priorities and choose the ones that are most important to you. You should consider those items that are most critical to *you* at this point in your life. As with all the activities in this book, it is important to be honest with yourself.

After reviewing the twenty-one blocks, create three columns. In the first column, place the seven blocks that you feel are your top priorities. In the next column, place the seven you would like to have if your first seven have been

Priority Blocks

Independence	Creativity	Influence
Help others	Respect	Security
Challenge	Make decisions	Adventure
Teamwork	Wealth	Relaxed pace
High pressure	Power	Use expertise
Exercise leadership	Public visibility	Precision work
Competition	Intellectual stimulation	Social contact

attained. Finally, in the third column, place the seven blocks that are the least important.

Now, review your Top Priority blocks, and make a quick assessment of how many are realized *to a reasonable degree* in your current work. If you find five to seven, consider yourself lucky. If you find three or less, it's time to consider some serious changes. If you find four, your satisfaction is likely to depend on the importance of the ones you don't have.

Next, list the priorities missing in your current work (if you

Top Priority	Would Enjoy Having	Least Important

have all the top seven, work with those in the second column), and work out a strategy for making each priority more of a reality. Consider such possibilities as restructuring your position, making a lateral transfer, or moving elsewhere.

Priority Planning

Priority

_____ Strategy _____

_____

_____ Strategy _____

_____

_____ Strategy _____

_____

_____ Strategy _____

_____

_____ Strategy _____

_____

_____ Strategy _____

_____

_____ Strategy _____

_____

Preferred Work Style

In most jobs, success requires the ability to approach a problem from a variety of perspectives, but some jobs are more demanding than others in certain areas. For example, most jobs in the helping professions and in sales require a reasonable amount of skill at interpersonal relations. Most jobs in product design, promotion, and planning require some degree of creativity. Jobs in financial services, bookkeeping, and ac-

counting emphasize practicality. Work in engineering, archi-
tecture, and manufacturing often requires a methodical orientation.

Each of us brings a certain way of doing things to our work.
In fact, we usually see people who don't do things our way as
less competent than ourselves. Actually, they may be equally
competent; the difference is simply their approach. Research
on the ways people learn suggests that the extent to which
people feel they are learning at work has an influence on the
way they feel about their jobs. It is significant that:

**When people stop learning
new things at work,
performance, motivation,
and therefore satisfaction decrease.**

If this is true—and there is overwhelming evidence that it
is—understanding your preferred style of learning and thus of
working can be an integral part of your career management.

Before discussing this important concept any further, I'd like
you to take a few minutes to complete a questionnaire on work
styles. To get the most out of this activity, don't try to second-
guess the meaning of your responses. There are no right or
wrong answers here. Answer honestly for an honest assessment of your personal work style.

Preferred Work Style Assessment Questionnaire

The following twenty-one questions will give you a quick and
easy assessment of your preferred style. In each case, circle
the response that most closely approximates the way you *really* are. Choose only *one* response for each question. Base your
response to each question on what you would do *first* in relation to that question.

1. If you are starting a new task at work, do you tend to:
   a. find out from others how it's done.
   b. imagine the final outcome.

    c. focus on the first step.

    d. outline all the steps before starting.

2. If you are trying to teach someone a new task and help them to feel comfortable with it, do you:

    a. have them try the first step.

    b. have them talk about how they feel about the task.

    c. have them imagine the outcome.

    d. help them develop a plan for completing the task.

3. If you are presented with a manual of a new problem area and told to study it, would you:

    a. read it from cover to cover.

    b. talk to others familiar with it as you read.

    c. scan it and read the most interesting parts.

    d. figure out what's most important and read that first.

4. If you and a co-worker had an argument, would you tend to:

    a. ignore them and do your own work.

    b. talk about your feelings with them.

    c. ask them to brainstorm alternatives with you.

    d. analyze the problem and decide who was right.

5. If someone you're working with is having a personal problem, do you tend to:

    a. ignore it.

    b. distract them by focusing on something else.

    c. talk with them about it.

    d. help them solve it.

6. If you were asked to create a budget for a project, would you:

    a. approximate costs.

    b. develop a system for pinpointing costs.

    c. find a similar budget for comparison.

    d. get direct quotes from vendors.

7. If you were given responsibility for appraising the performance of subordinates, would you:

    a. complete a brief questionnaire on each one periodically.

    b. hold regular meetings with them to discuss performance.

    c. work with them to establish a system of appraisal.

    d. implement a comprehensive performance management system that measures every aspect of their performance.

8. If the equipment you're working with breaks down, do you:

    a. try to fix it yourself.

    b. ask advice from people around you.

    c. call the repair shop.

    d. find out if it happens often.

9. At committee meetings, do you tend to:

    a. get involved in conversation.

    b. observe the group.

    c. maintain order.

    d. focus the group's attention on the problem at hand.

10. If the committee you're working on is not getting the job done, do you tend to:

    a. stop showing up.

    b. get the group to rethink the task.

    c. suggest a new approach to solving the problem.

    d. discuss the group's process and its impact on the completion of the task.

11. Given the choice of working alone or on a team, would you:

    a. choose to work alone.

   b. talk to potential teammates to get a feel for their attitudes before deciding.

   c. choose to work on a team.

   d. examine the backgrounds of potential teammates before deciding.

12. If your boss suddenly took ill, would you:
   a. keep doing what you were doing.
   b. see how others felt about it.
   c. offer to follow through on his/her projects.
   d. get people to volunteer to help on projects.

13. If your organization was suddenly bought out or incorporated into a larger organization, would you:
   a. outline a plan for how they could use you.
   b. begin talking with the new bosses about your role.
   c. continue doing good work.
   d. think about options for you in the new organization.

14. If you were asked to describe what your responsibilities are to new management, would you:
   a. give them a formal report.
   b. talk with them about it informally.
   c. show them.
   d. ask them to complete a small assignment typical of your work.

15. If you were asked to join a union, would you:
   a. find out what others think about it.
   b. ask to see its track record.
   c. ask about the benefits.
   d. ask to be a guest at a union meeting.

16. If you were interviewing someone for a position in your organization, would you tend to focus on their:
   a. style of interaction.
   b. prior experience.

    c. problem-solving skills.

    d. understanding of themselves.

17. If you were forced to fire someone, would you focus first on:

    a. getting them the best-possible severance package.

    b. making sure they had plenty of personal support.

    c. helping them figure out what to do next.

    d. making sure you've carefully documented the process.

18. When faced with an unreasonable deadline, do you tend to:

    a. talk about it to relieve the pressure.

    b. do as much as you can as quickly as you can.

    c. try to find a quicker way to do the task.

    d. ask others to help.

19. If you were to start your own business, would you:

    a. thoroughly research the field first.

    b. start small and build up.

    c. focus on promotion and marketing.

    d. find a unique market niche and dive in.

20. If you were suddenly fired, would you:

    a. immediately start looking for new work.

    b. talk the situation over with your boss.

    c. brainstorm possible options.

    d. retrace the steps leading up to it to see if the damage could be undone.

21. When answering questionnaires such as this one, do you tend to:

    a. choose the response that feels right.

    b. finish as quickly as possible.

    c. look for a pattern to the response sequence.

    d. try to figure out what it all means.

Scoring

To determine your preferred work style, circle the response you gave for each question. Next, add the number of responses for each column. Your highest score indicates your preferred style.

Question	Interactive	Practical	Creative	Methodical
1	A	C	B	D
2	B	A	C	D
3	B	D	C	A
4	B	A	C	D
5	C	A	B	D
6	A	D	C	B
7	B	A	C	D
8	B	C	A	D
9	A	D	B	C
10	D	A	B	C
11	B	A	C	D
12	B	A	D	C
13	B	C	D	A
14	B	C	D	A
15	A	C	D	B
16	A	C	D	B
17	B	A	C	D
18	A	B	D	C
19	D	B	C	A
20	B	A	C	D
21	A	B	D	C

TOTALS _____   _____   _____   _____

Score Analysis: A high score in any one column (8 or above) means that this style is a strong preference. Two close scores or a tie indicates a strong secondary style as well as a primary style. To break a tie, read the descriptions in the Style Explanation Chart and see which of the two styles best fits the way you operate.

What It All Means

The Preferred Work Style Model is a tool for understanding your behavior at work. It is one of several models based on research in learning styles conducted by David Kolb at Case Western Reserve University. Although these various models differ in scope and perspective, there are a few things to keep in mind about them all:

- No style is inherently better than any other.
- Each style has its strengths and weaknesses.
- Though we all use all the styles to varying degrees, each of us has a preferred style.

Now, keeping these points in mind, take a few minutes to read about your preferred style on the Style Explanation Chart.

Implications of Preferred Style

The concept of preferred work style has many implications. The one that is most relevant here concerns matching your job/role with your preferred style. People engaged in work that does not allow them to use their preferred style *to a reasonable degree* generally become very frustrated. In addition, there are important implications for work relationships and organizational success.

The Significance of Style in Managing Relationships

My best example of the importance of understanding style in a working relationship is a personal one. My preferred style is creative; my wife's preferred style is methodical. We go camping for three weeks every summer. On my way home from work that last day before vacation, I click into my creative style and start visualizing our campsite all set up and the two of us walking on the beach. When I get home, this translates into my throwing everything into the car as quickly as possible so that we can realize my fantasy. My wife comes out and stops me

Style Explanation Chart

INTERACTIVE

- Good initiator
- Uses intuition
- Draws others out
- Motivates others
- Looks for new angles
- Thrives on change
- Good at adapting
- Willing to risk
- Likes working in groups
- Sensitive to others' needs

CREATIVE

- Sees the big picture
- Appreciates aesthetics
- Uses all senses for understanding situations
- Good at visualizing possibilities
- Good at observing and seeing through things
- Is supportive of others
- Tends to be very calm
- Good at modeling behavior
- Uses imagination
- Good listener

PRACTICAL

- Good at getting results
- Applies theories
- Solves concrete problems well
- Takes control
- Acts independently
- Relies on facts
- Uses trial and error
- Is unemotional
- Good at testing ideas
- Likes to get things done

METHODICAL

- Good at planning
- Is very careful
- Is very organized
- Is thorough
- Works independently
- Relies on rationality
- Develops ideas
- Builds theories
- Thinks ahead
- Is very deliberate

cold. Operating according to her preferred style (methodical), she informs me of her plan to pack the car strategically so that setting up camp will be more efficient. An argument ensues. Finally, I say, "I know what the problem is. I'm being creative; you're being methodical." She says, "No, I'm being reasonable; you're being a pain in the ass!" (A fresh perspective always helps.)

We are in fact operating in different styles. From her perspective, I am being a pain for interfering with the orderly process she has in mind that *would* make the trip easier. She, in turn, is interfering with my desire to get away as quickly as possible. Neither of us is right or wrong; we just bring different perspectives to the situation. Once that becomes clear, the solution is easy. I haul the equipment out of the house; she packs the car.

The Significance of Style in Organizational Life

**For organizational success,
diversity is the spice of life.**

At some point in their lives, most people can't help thinking that life would be better if more people saw the world the way they do. In reality, organizations would be a lot less successful if everyone had the same preferred work style. Imagine, for a moment, what a totally homogeneous organization might look like.

Interactive: a lot of care taking, nurturing of relationships, and a lot of conversation, but not a lot of results.

Creative: a lot of long-range planning, innovative ideas, and a lot of vision for the future, but not a lot of concrete activity.

Methodical: a lot of strategizing, planning, and problem solving, but not much attention to how people are managed.

Practical: a lot of projects completed, but lack of a sense of overall purpose and attention to people.

Fortunately, most organizations realize the need for people who play different roles. In making career decisions, it is important to pay attention to the organization, the department, or the division you're considering entering. Make sure there's room in it for someone with your preferred style, or you may find yourself a round peg in a square hole or, worse, a round peg in a sea of other round pegs with nothing unique to offer.

Exploring Interests

A key area in exploring options is, of course, interests. Many of your interests should be reflected in the work you do and in the skills and knowledge you have acquired. The purpose of this activity is to uncover some interests that may be a bit more subtle or hidden by preoccupation with the demands of day-to-day life. A plaque given to a colleague of mine captures the spirit of such a quest:

The task of life is to do that which we would have done before someone told us we had to make a living.

I have developed a list of questions intended to uncover some of those hidden or forgotten interests.

Interest Inventory

Answer the following questions with as many responses as come to mind (search for at least *two* responses to each question). For now, do not concern yourself with whether or not your responses are related to work.

1. Think of a colleague you admire. What do you find appealing about that person's work?

   a. _____

   b. _____

2. Think of a relative whose work you respect. What do you find appealing about that person's work?

   a. _____

   b. _____

3. Think of the last movie or television show that really held your interest. What was it about the program that kept you involved?

   a. _____

   b. _____

4. If you could choose a different educational background or field of study, what might it be?

   a. _____

   b. _____

5. Imagine yourself a skilled journalist in charge of a major newspaper section. What section(s) might you choose?

   a. _____

   b. _____

6. Imagine yourself independently wealthy yet interested in running your own business. What might that business be?

   a. _____

   b. _____

7. When you think about issues or conditions in the world, which ones make you the most angry and/or excited? What is it about each of these that gets you going?

   a. _____

   b. _____

Once you have at least fourteen responses to the seven questions, study your results, and circle the seven items of interest that you find *most compelling*—that is, the ones to which you are the most drawn.

Competencies

In managing your career, being keenly aware of your strengths is critical both to your performance on the job and to your career mobility. This section will focus on two distinct yet overlapping areas: your knowledge and your skills. We will use the following definitions to distinguish the two:

Knowledge area: Subject matter you know about
Skill: Something you can do
A skill plus a knowledge area equals a **competency**
Here are some examples:
A good French teacher would:
    a. know French (knowledge area).
    b. be able to teach (skill).
A good carpenter would:
    a. understand the properties of wood (knowledge area).
    b. be able to handle tools (skill).
A good tax accountant would:
    a. be familiar with tax law (knowledge area).
    b. be adept at mathematics (skill).

Rather than rely on your current awareness of your skills and knowledge areas, I am going to ask you to use a technique for jarring your memory. This activity involves scanning your history and identifying events in your life in which you played a key role. The only other requirements are that you:

    a. perceive you did the job well.
    b. received some satisfaction from it, either during the activity or in retrospect.

In the following review, list three significant events for each time period. Here are some examples to get you going:

- Built a go-cart
- Won a spelling bee
- Performed in the school play
- Played in a rock band
- Wrote a poem
- Solved a production problem
- Redesigned a filing system
- Organized a fund drive
- Sold a record number of products
- Designed a new computer program

Significant Events Review

Ages 7–10

1. _____
2. _____
3. _____

Ages 11–13

1. _____
2. _____
3. _____

Ages 14–17

1. _____
2. _____
3. _____

Ages 18–21

1. _____

2. _____

3. _____

Ages 22–24

1. _____

2. _____

3. _____

Ages 25–27

1. _____

2. _____

3. _____

Ages 28–30

1. _____

2. _____

3. _____

Ages 31–34

1. _____

2. _____

3. _____

Ages 35–37

1. _____

2. _____

3. _____

Ages 38–40

1. _____
2. _____
3. _____

Ages 41–43

1. _____
2. _____
3. _____

Ages 44–47

1. _____
2. _____
3. _____

Ages 48–50

1. _____
2. _____
3. _____

Ages 51–53

1. _____
2. _____
3. _____

Ages 54–56

1. _____
2. _____
3. _____

Ages 57–59

1. _____
2. _____
3. _____

Ages 60 and Above

1. _____
2. _____
3. _____

Knowledge Scan

Now that you have reviewed the significant events in your life, you have a ready reference from which to extract your knowledge areas. Look over the list briefly, and think about the knowledge you *used or gained* in each of your significant events; then complete the Knowledge Inventory below.

Definition of Knowledge Levels

For each of the following categories, list at least eight knowledge areas. Use your list of significant events as your guide, but do not limit yourself to those items. If you think of others along the way, use them as well.

Expert: You know more than most other people about this. (Don't be modest.)

Working knowledge: You don't know as much as some, but you've got a pretty good grasp.

Dabbled in: You've taken a course, read a book, or played around with this subject matter.

Knowledge Inventory

Expert

_____

_____

_____

_____

_____

_____

_____

_____

Working knowledge

_____

_____

_____

_____

_____

_____

_____

Dabbled in

_____

_____

_____

_____

_____

_____

_____

_____

Once you've completed the Knowledge Inventory, study your list, and circle your strongest knowledge areas—three from expert, three from working knowledge, and two from dabbled in—for a total of eight items.

Skills Review

You are now ready to examine your skills. If you remove the knowledge or information from a competency, you are left with what might be called _generic skills_—abilities that, when coupled with various forms of information, become marketable talents. Once again, breaking the skills down into their parts will help you to understand them.

Think of skills in three categories:

Skills of the heart: These skills have to do with people and require the use of emotion and intuition.

Skills of the head: These skills have to do with information and require the use of intellect and rationality.

Skills of the hands: These skills have to do with things and require manual dexterity and physical adeptness.

Skills Inventory

Check the appropriate items on the following list, using your significant events as a frame of reference but also including other experiences you think of. Note that you are being asked to consider each item from two perspectives:

a. Those you enjoy and are willing to continue using.
b. Those you do well based on prior experience.

SKILLS OF THE HEART

	Enjoy and Am Willing to Continue Using	Do Well Based on Prior Experience
1. Communicating		
Talking to individuals	_____	_____
Talking to groups	_____	_____
Writing correspondence	_____	_____
Writing business materials	_____	_____
Writing creatively	_____	_____
Listening	_____	_____
2. Teaching/Training		
Designing educational/ training materials	_____	_____
Motivating people	_____	_____
Leading groups	_____	_____
Creating an effective learning environment	_____	_____
Demonstrating ideas through example and illustration	_____	_____
Evaluating program effectiveness	_____	_____

	Enjoy and Am Willing to Continue Using	*Do Well Based on Prior Experience*

3. Managing/Supervising

Setting goals and objectives   _____   _____

Organizing people   _____   _____

Engendering trust   _____   _____

Building a team   _____   _____

Designing projects   _____   _____

Delegating authority   _____   _____

4. Influencing/Persuading

Negotiating   _____   _____

Managing conflict   _____   _____

Compromising   _____   _____

Collaborating   _____   _____

Competing   _____   _____

Bargaining   _____   _____

5. Counseling/Consulting

Caring for others   _____   _____

Giving feedback   _____   _____

Mentoring   _____   _____

Inspiring others   _____   _____

Solving people problems   _____   _____

Giving advice   _____   _____

	Enjoy and Am Willing to Continue Using	Do Well Based on Prior Experience

SKILLS OF THE HEAD

6. Problem Solving/Decision Making

	Enjoy and Am Willing to Continue Using	Do Well Based on Prior Experience
Clarifying problems	_____	_____
Evaluating alternatives	_____	_____
Generating solutions	_____	_____
Assessing feasibility	_____	_____
Testing ideas	_____	_____
Determining outcomes	_____	_____

7. Organizing

Designing systems	_____	_____
Classifying information	_____	_____
Coordinating resources	_____	_____
Monitoring progress	_____	_____
Synthesizing ideas	_____	_____
Streamlining procedures	_____	_____

8. Planning

Setting policies	_____	_____
Developing alternatives	_____	_____
Choosing direction	_____	_____
Outlining procedures	_____	_____
Researching alternatives	_____	_____
Assessing and adjusting priorities	_____	_____

	Enjoy and Am Willing to Continue Using	*Do Well Based on Prior Experience*
9. Creating		
Imagining/visualizing concepts	_____	_____
Creating new ideas	_____	_____
Creating new images	_____	_____
Inventing new products	_____	_____
Using intuition	_____	_____
Conceiving new interpretations	_____	_____
10. Computing		
Accounting	_____	_____
Keeping records	_____	_____
Managing budgets	_____	_____
Interpreting data	_____	_____
Word processing	_____	_____
Monitoring inventory flow	_____	_____

SKILLS OF THE HANDS

	Enjoy and Am Willing to Continue Using	*Do Well Based on Prior Experience*
11. Mechanical		
Operating equipment	_____	_____
Repairing equipment	_____	_____
Assembling equipment	_____	_____
Monitoring equipment performance	_____	_____
Maintaining equipment	_____	_____

	Enjoy and Am Willing to Continue Using	Do Well Based on Prior Experience

12. Athletic

Building and maintaining endurance	____	____
Using eye-hand coordination	____	____
Excelling in a sport	____	____
Demonstrating agility	____	____
Demonstrating physical flexibility	____	____
Demonstrating physical strength	____	____

13. Physical

Maintaining good health	____	____
Maintaining physical fitness	____	____
Demonstrating fine motor coordination	____	____
Using tools	____	____
Doing precision work	____	____
Assembling structures	____	____

14. Technical

Reading blueprints	____	____
Managing energy systems	____	____
Navigating direction	____	____
Analyzing potential dysfunction	____	____
Understanding specifications	____	____
Regulating controls	____	____

	Enjoy and Am Willing to Continue Using	*Do Well Based on Prior Experience*

15. *Natural*

Tending animals	_____	_____
Tending plants	_____	_____
Monitoring environmental conditions	_____	_____
Testing natural resources	_____	_____
Monitoring growth	_____	_____
Resolving organic problems	_____	_____
Manipulating the physical world	_____	_____

Notice that there were fifteen numbered categories in the skills checklist. Review the list, considering the categories with the most checks first. Then identify the five numbered areas that represent your strongest skills—that is, the ones you both use well and enjoy using—and list them here.

Five strongest skill categories

1. _____
2. _____
3. _____
4. _____
5. _____

Preferred Workplace Culture

**Eighty percent of positions vacated
through voluntary or involuntary means
are a result of people not fitting in.**

This statistic, suggested by research conducted by the U.S. Department of Labor, Bureau of Labor Statistics, has strong implications for career management. If, indeed, the cause for dismissal or resignation has less to do with competence than with environment, understanding workplace culture and choosing one that provides a good match for you are essential.

Sheila S.: From Academic to Entrepreneur

Sheila had spent two years teaching writing at the college level and working on her doctoral dissertation on various aspects of technical and expository writing. She came to see me because she felt doubtful about commiting the *next* two years to the completion of her dissertation and wondered whether she was on the right track.

After several conversations, it became increasingly clear that she was fed up with her role as writing critic for her students and writing foil (her term) for her doctoral committee. She was dissatisfied with the intellectual culture she was immersed in. What she really wanted was to apply her considerable talents where they would be truly appreciated. The idea of making more money also appealed to her.

After completing her CareerMap Profile, she decided that she needed an entrepreneurial environment in which she could use her formidable writing skills and be well paid for them. She eventually got a job in midtown Manhattan doing promotional writing for a public relations firm. Although she puts in sixteen-hour days, she loves the work, finds the people really exciting, and relishes the fact that *her* revisions are the final ones.

The difference for Sheila is that now she uses her skills in an environment that stimulates her and toward an end that makes sense to her.

Choosing a Workplace Culture

Although you may not always be able to choose the exact culture you'd like to work in, you can establish some guidelines. As you do the next exercise, remember that it is not uncommon to find several cultures within a single organization. Don't despair if you find you're currently mismatched; a lateral move may cure your ills.

Culture Constellation

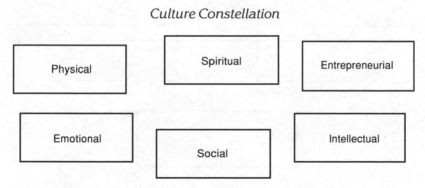

Study this Culture Constellation, and spend some time considering what you think each culture might be like. Then look below and read the definitions of each culture for further clarification.

Culture Definitions

Physical: an environment that emphasizes achieving results through stretching physical limits.

Spiritual: an environment that emphasizes creating and maintaining a sense of spiritual and ethical standards for the organization.

Entrepreneurial: an environment that emphasizes perpetu-
ating the growth and profitability of the organization.
Emotional: an environment that emphasizes meeting the
personal and psychological needs of people.
Social: an environment that emphasizes achieving goals
through the interaction of organizational members.
Intellectual: an environment that emphasizes pursuing the
frontiers of knowledge and breaking new ground.

Most environments are made up of a mix of cultural characteristics. Review the Culture Constellation once again,
choose the *three* types of cultures in which you would most
like to work, and place them in the Personal Culture Cluster.

Personal Culture Cluster

Career Visualization—More Than Coincidence

**If you can't imagine yourself
doing something,
there's a good chance
you will never do it.**

I used to be skeptical of stories on the power of the mind to
influence future events. Over the years, though, my attitude

has been changed by my own experience, the experiences of people I know, and the beliefs of people I respect. I've seen countless examples of people who visualize success and then attain it. They use visualization to fortify a belief in their abilities, almost as a form of self-hypnosis.

**Trying to make someone believe in you
when you don't believe in yourself is
like trying to make an atheist
repent for his/her sins.**

My most personal experience with visualization was watching my wife almost effortlessly (from my perspective) give birth to our son while so many around us struggled in agony. When I asked her, much later, how she did it, she said she simply looked inward and visualized him in her arms.

Those of you who prefer to find answers in science might enjoy reading esteemed surgeon Bernie Siegel's work on the power of the mind over the body and the impact of visualization on patient recovery. In his book *Love, Medicine, and Miracles*, Dr. Siegel reports on one study that used imagery to predict patient recovery. By analyzing visualizations of their illnesses drawn by 200 patients, researchers were able to predict with 95 percent accuracy who would survive and who would not. The study of the relationship between the mind and the body has become so respectable that the National Institute of Mental Health recently held a three-day conference to discuss it. Dr. Siegel claims that in ten years, nearly all doubt about the power of visualization will have disappeared.

Those of you enamored of athletic prowess can read Bill Russell's story of how, when the Boston Celtics were really hot, he could actually see a play occur moments before it did. Or read *Inner Tennis, Inner Golf,* or *Inner Running* to hear masters in these sports attest to the power of visualization.

To successfully orchestrate your career, you need to have faith in your ability to do so, and one way to achieve that faith is to visualize yourself doing what you would like to do.

Visualization Exercise: A Typical Workday

This next and last step in Profile development will help you to develop your ability to visualize your ideal career. To do it, you need to find a comfortable position and five quiet minutes.

Once you've found the position and the time, take a quick inventory of your body, noting any parts that feel particularly tense: your back, your neck, and so on. To relax yourself, slowly tense those muscles even more and then gradually relax them. Repeat this with all your tension spots until your body is completely relaxed.

In a moment, I am going to ask you to close your eyes and visualize. There is nothing mysterious about this act; simply read the suggestions, close your eyes, and allow it to happen.

For the next five minutes, imagine you are experiencing a typical workday five years in the future, a time when you have attained your ideal work situation. Allow your mind to move through this day, focusing in particular on the following aspects:

- What precisely are you doing?
- In what type of environment?
- Working with:
  - skills of the heart?
  - skills of the head?
  - skills of the hands?
- Toward what end?

Keeping these four considerations in focus, close your eyes and begin.

Once you've finished, answer the questions in the Work Visualization Analysis.

Work Visualization Analysis

1. What type of work were you doing? _____
   _____
   _____

2. In what type of physical environment were you working? _____
   _____

3. In what type of culture were you working? _____

_____

4. What skills of the heart were you using? _____

_____

_____

5. What skills of the head? _____

_____

_____

6. What skills of the hands? _____

_____

_____

7. Toward what end were you working? _____

_____

_____

Your CareerMap Profile

Congratulations! You have finished the arduous but necessary task of examining your needs, desires, abilities, and priorities for charting your own future.

The next task is a simple organizational one. On page 55, you'll find a blueprint for your own CareerMap Profile. Match the headings on the Profile sheet with the headings in this chapter to plug your personal information into the spaces provided.

Once you complete development of your CareerMap Profile, turn to Chapter 3 to find out how you can use it to develop options that will lead to making your career ambitions a reality.

THE CAREERMAP PROFILE OF

_____
(your name)

Personal Priorities   *Preferred Work Style*

_____   _____
_____
_____
_____

_____

_____

Interests   *Knowledge Areas*

_____   _____

_____   _____

_____   _____

_____   _____

_____   _____

_____   _____

Skill Areas   *Personal Culture Cluster*

_____   _____

_____   _____

_____   _____

_____

Visualization (summary)

_____

_____

THREE

Developing Your Options/Making Tough Choices

Having It All

WE LIVE in an unprecedented age of options. Although this has its advantages, the range of available career choices can sometimes be overwhelming, so much so that the careful consideration of options becomes a skill in itself. This chapter focuses on developing that skill by presenting strategies for generating options and then narrowing them effectively.

Raymond L.: A Kid in a Candy Store

Raymond L. came to see me in the spring of 1985. Independently wealthy, Raymond had a problem that was a little different from most. Ever since he was a child, Raymond has received a weekly check equivalent to that of a well-paid executive. As a result of this financial freedom, he spent his early adult years accumulating various college degrees and dabbling in a number of areas.

About to turn forty, Raymond suddenly realized he had no sense of direction. He could do virtually anything he wanted, but he didn't know what to do. Part of his problem—and this is where Raymond is very much like the rest of us—is that he had a limited view of his options. He didn't want to be an accountant, a teacher, or a lawyer, and he was at a lost for ideas.

After several conversations and a review of his CareerMap Profile, Raymond decided to channel his efforts in three directions: He would continue managing his end of the family business, grow exotic vegetables, and begin writing children's books. He is currently doing all three and finds himself challenged in the physical, entrepreneurial, and intellectual realms (his personal culture cluster).

Although the rest of us may not be in Raymond's position financially, we can learn from his experience. First, his dilemma is an example of the way most people fail to see beyond the obvious possibilities. Second, Raymond's shifting roles reflect the changing notion of career stability. Two well-established trends are echoed in this example: Most people will change careers four to six times during their lifetime, and an increasing number of people will split their efforts among several part-time endeavors. (In a special report on the economy of the 1990s, *Fortune* magazine (Feb. 2, 1987) recently reported that an estimated 20 percent of jobs created in the 1990s will be part-time positions.)

Each of these trends could have a significant impact on your career management. The likelihood that four to six major changes will occur for most people suggests that:

**There is no such thing as the perfect job;
there is only the next good job.**

Reactions to this statistic range from terror to joy. Those who revel in change find this inevitable state of flux a cause for celebration; others find the idea paralyzing. However, it is possible to transform the terror into acceptance, if not joy.

One obstacle to accepting the fluidity of the career marketplace and to developing a rich pool of options is the notion of *having it all*. We all know people who, in pursuit of having it all, find themselves instead on the verge of having a nervous breakdown. Consider this:

**You can have it all,
but maybe not all at once.**

I recently met with a woman who began our conversation with: "I want a job in a new field that pays as much as my current job, is within fifteen miles of my home, allows me to utilize all my strongest skills, gives me three weeks of vacation, is exciting, and is secure." I politely told her I couldn't help her and suggested that she come back when she had given up some of her requirements.

**Nothing closes doors more quickly
than a closed mind.**

The Awful Truth

Most people I have worked with have realized the importance of an open mind and have recognized that the key to a satisfying life is making choices about what they want most at *this* point in their lives. I have met others who work to avoid making such choices. For such people:

**The American Dream becomes
the nightmare of the unattainable.**

We all know people who are seduced by the notion that the world should be at their fingertips. Their credit cards are always at the limit. Their relationships are strained. Their children, if they have any, are more familiar with the baby-sitter than their parents. Their health is at risk; their therapy bills are exorbitant; and they are always busy. If you recognize yourself here, take heart. Many people like you have overcome this confusion through a careful realignment of their priorities. Here are just a few examples of the people I've watched redirect their lives through a shift in careers:

Leo M. left a high-paying management position to teach high school math. Tired of the pressure cooker environ-

ment and on financially stable ground, he chose a chance
to contribute to others' education and a saner schedule
over what he called the "manufacturing grind."

Diane S. left what she called the "dull drone" of teaching
for the intellectual stimulation of designing tests at a
national testing firm.

Gail C. was brave enough to admit that she was tired of
being a "bleeding heart" and left human services for a
lucrative real estate career.

Kelly D. was a very successful commodities broker who
left her job temporarily to raise her children.

Larry R. took a job as a city housing director despite his
successful real estate development business. He said,
"I wanted to use my skills to help something other than
my pocketbook."

These people chose options that made their lives saner by
their own standards. The key to their success—and they all
feel tremendously successful—lies in giving up priorities that
had come to mean less to them than new ones that more
accurately reflected their current needs and desires. As you
begin generating options, keep in mind what you want and
need *most* at this point in your life.

Generating Options: Forming a CORE Group

Once you've completed your CareerMap Profile (Chapter
2), you have three choices: You can sit at home and contem-
plate a move (a lonely choice). You can pay someone several thousand dollars to tell you what you should do (an
expensive choice). Or you can utilize your network of contacts (we *all* have them) to create a personal think tank—
what I call a CORE (Career Options Response Effort) Group—
to work on your strategy. A CORE Group is a small group of

people gathered specifically to help you identify your options. Obviously, I find this third choice the wisest. However, your CORE Group must be formed carefully, or it will not produce what you need.

**An effective CORE Group looks more
like an ad hoc (special-purpose)
committee than a support group.**

Support groups, while great for support, are generally not a good source of ideas. Many of my clients, after completing a seminar series, form follow-up support groups to help them with the period of transition. These groups are helpful—indeed, some last for years—but their focus generally shifts rather quickly from career to personal concerns. This is to be expected, since 80 percent of the people I work with in career transition also report being in transition in some other aspect of their lives.

The point is: If you're looking for ideas, pursue ideas. Also, be aware that your usual supports—spouse, close friends, relatives—may be the wrong people for your CORE Group; they have too much invested in the outcome and too many notions about what would be good for you. Now, keeping these pitfalls in mind, you're ready to form your CORE Group.

CORE Group Formation Guidelines

1. Make a list of the ten best minds you know (try to get a diverse group), and ask them if they would be willing to spend an hour thinking about your career with you. Be sure to let them know you want only one hour of their time.

2. Once you have five to eight willing participants, get a bottle of wine (or sparkling cider) and a comfortable place to meet.

3. Before the meeting, transfer your CareerMap Profile to a large sheet of paper so it will be easily readable when hung on the wall.

4. Begin by giving the group a brief explanation of how you developed the Profile, and ask them to brain-storm possible options for you, based on what they see in the Profile. Be sure to make the following points:

   • The goal is to come up with as many ideas as possible. (Stop at fifty items or sixty minutes, whichever comes first; I've never seen fewer than forty items appear.)

   • There should be no self-censorship, regardless of how outrageous, boring, or impractical an idea might seem. (Such ideas sometimes lead to the most promising options.)

   • The host (you) will not comment except to add items to the list or to ask the group to expand its range (e.g., consider self-employment, a shift within the current organization, or a shift in arenas).

5. Ask someone to record all the options elicited from the group. (Provide an additional sheet of paper and a marker so that everyone can see the developing list.)

6. Turn them loose, and listen.

7. Write follow-up letters thanking them for their help and letting them know what came of the activity.

Sample Profile for CORE Group Consideration
CareerMap Profile of Leslie Winston

Personal Priorities

Creativity
Influence
Independence
Social contact
Wealth
Respect
Challenge

Preferred Work Style

Methodical

Interests

International trade
Economics
Travel
History
Novels
Politics
Tennis

Knowledge Areas

Insurance
Stock market
Personnel policies
Accounting
Sales
Gourmet cooking
Creative financing
Sailing

Skill Areas

Managing/supervising
Problem solving/
decision making
Planning
Computing
Technical

Personal Culture Cluster

Entrepreneurial
Social
Intellectual

Visualization Summary

Working with a small group of highly professional colleagues. Doing work that draws on my technical expertise and my ability to see the "less than obvious" and that gives me a chance to be innovative.

Sorting Your Options

As Raymond's story demonstrated, being unable to eliminate options is as debilitating as not having enough choices.
Your CORE Group has given you a list of options. (If you're
not satisfied with the list, you may want to recall the group or
form a new one.) The next task is to identify those options
you want to pursue. Unless you've hit on exactly what you
want to do at this point, you need to weed out the definite nos
and zero in on the most promising alternatives. The best way
to do this is to categorize your forty-plus alternatives into
four groups.

Sort 1

The first column is for those ideas not even worth consideration. Remember, in deference to your CORE Group and their
potential creativity, you didn't censor these when they first
emerged; now is the time to get rid of them. Place all the
ideas you find truly awful in the Awful column. Next, put the
ideas that sound really fantastic in the Wonderful column.
Now, place the ideas that are not overwhelming but might be
worth pursuing in the Interesting column. Finally, put those
ideas that you don't yet know enough about but that might
be possibilities if you knew more in the Mysterious column.

Awful	Wonderful	Interesting	Mysterious
_____	_____	_____	_____
_____	_____	_____	_____
_____	_____	_____	_____
_____	_____	_____	_____
_____	_____	_____	_____
_____	_____	_____	_____
_____	_____	_____	_____

Awful	*Wonderful*	*Interesting*	*Mysterious*
_____	_____	_____	_____
_____	_____	_____	_____
_____	_____	_____	_____

Sample Sort 1

Awful	*Wonderful*	*Interesting*	*Mysterious*
Write historical novels	Run a tennis camp	Real estate appraiser	Corporate risk analyst
Teach accounting at a community college	Real estate developer	Insurance appraiser	Financial planner
Make cooking videotapes	Bank loan officer	Computer analyst	Estate liquidator
Travel agent	Independent human resource consultant	Sell computer systems	Outward Bound leader
Computer programmer	International trade consultant	Stockbroker	Title search business
Teach college economics	Market and direct business cruises	Start a direct-mail marketing firm	Public relations business
Continue as manager of underwriting	Work for political analysis firm	Import/export business	Literary agent
Budget counselor	Run a charter cruise business	Manage a personal computer store	Advertising executive
Teach high school math	Own and manage an exclusive inn	Run a temporary personnel agency	Sports accessory product development
Manage a chain of laundromats	Manage an international sports magazine	Executive recruiter	Lobbyist
			Professional fund raiser

Sort 2

At this stage, you need to review the mysterious ideas and figure out what you need to do to make them less mysterious (e.g., read about them, talk to people about them). See Occupational Investigation in the POINT Process in Chapter 6 for details on how to do this. Research these ideas until you feel confident with putting them in the Wonderful, Interesting, or Awful column.

Once you have reorganized your options, you need to narrow them. Begin by eliminating 50 percent of your items in the Wonderful column and 50 percent of the items in the Interesting column. Do this by sorting the ten (or so) items in each column into two groups: strong and weak. Discard the weak and list the strong, along with the mysterious items still under consideration, on the Sort 2 work sheet.

Once you've discarded the Awful choices, demystified the Mysterious choices (or decided which ones you want to demystify), and narrowed your Wonderful and Interesting options, your list should look like this:

Wonderful Ideas   *Interesting Ideas*

_____   _____

_____   _____

_____   _____

_____   _____

_____   _____

_____   _____

_____   _____

_____   _____

Sample Sort 2

Wonderful Ideas	*Interesting Ideas*
Real estate developer	Real estate appraiser
Independent human resource consultant	Insurance appraiser
Political analyst	Title search business
Outward Bound leader	Computer analyst
Corporate risk analyst	Financial planner
International trade consultant	Manage a personal computer store

Sort 3

The next step is to narrow the remaining options toward a course of action. There is no special technique for doing this; simply consider the possibilities, and decide what you want to do. If at this point you find yourself unable to move, turn to Chapters 4 and 5, which address the two most common obstacles to making important moves: fear of change and fear of risk. If you find yourself raring to go by this time, you may want to skip to Chapter 6 and begin moving through the POINT Process.

Before you do either, however, make sure you narrow your options to a field of four (two from the Wonderful column and two from the Interesting column). Use these four items as your frame of reference for the chapters that follow.

Wonderful	*Interesting*
_____	_____
_____	_____

Sample Sort 3

Wonderful	*Interesting*
Independent human resource consultant	Financial planner
Corporate risk analyst	Computer analyst

PART 2

TAKING OFF

FOUR

Clearing the Runway: Overcoming Obstacles to Change

IN TODAY'S marketplace, one thing is certain: Change is inevitable. Companies, hospitals, schools, and agencies will go out of business or, worse, will be ineffective if they do not accept the presence of change in everyday life. The ways in which organizations manage change are critical to their survival. The ways in which individuals manage their own transitions in the context of organizational change are a key to *their* survival. This chapter discusses various obstacles to creating change and offers strategies for overcoming those obstacles.

A Dozen Deadly Demons and the Twelve Disciples of Change

Change makes people uncomfortable. Given the chance, most will go to great lengths to avoid it. Once participants in my seminars have identified their goals, I ask them what excuses they come up with to stop themselves from pursuing their desires and to avoid the discomfort that accompanies change. Here are twelve of the most common, most debilitating excuses and some strategies for combating them.

The forces that propel and prevent change are so strong I refer to them as *demons* and *disciples*. The demon bears the message of defeat: that you shouldn't even bother trying. The disciple bears the message of success: that you have nothing to lose and everything to gain. To successfully orchestrate change and effectively manage your career, you need to exorcise the demons and embrace the disciples.

Lack of Opportunity

Demon 1
There aren't many good opportunities out there, so why bother.

Disciple 1
**A good job is like a good lover:
You only need one.**

One of the first things I tell my clients is to stop paying attention to the statistics. A friend recently told me that "there are only twenty-four hundred people in this country who make a living through their writing." As a writer, I have two choices. The first is to say to myself, "Well, then, I'll never be able to make it as a writer." In that case, I will probably be right. The second is to say to myself, "If I am going to succeed at this, I have to be truly committed to it." I have to ask myself, "Is it worth it?" If I decide that it is and to go ahead with my writing, the meaning of the statistic becomes, "Achieving this goal will be worthwhile and will make me part of a very select group." This new interpretation turns a potential obstacle into a benefit and frees me to pursue my goal wholeheartedly.

You are more likely to be exposed to typical jobs performed by thousands of people than to unique jobs performed by a select few. Because you see fewer people in the more specialized positions, you may tend to think of these positions as beyond reach. But there are unique opportunities everywhere; it's simply a matter of considering what you are capable of doing.

Another belief about opportunities that gets in the way is that people who hold esteemed positions "know the truth." It amazes me how often people choose to abandon a goal because of a single person's opinion.

Brenda B.: A Design for Designing

Brenda B. was totally lost when she came to my seminar. She had a degree in Middle Eastern studies and few job experiences she cared to recall. No longer interested in the Middle East—her choice of subject had had more to do with a need for an undergraduate major than with a passion for the Middle East—she couldn't decide what to pursue. She had accepted the limits of her current marketability and was prepared to return to school; she was open to almost anything.

One striking aspect about her was her impeccable dress, with fine attention to detail, coordination, and fashion. Each week, she received compliments from both women and men about how attractive she looked. During a brainstorming session, someone suggested an option that got her really excited—fashion design. Her Profile echoed the intuitive responses of the group, showing that she valued innovation, fast pace, and creativity; that she had skills in conceptualizing, problem solving, and organizing; and that she was interested in anything that had to do with clothing. After brainstorming and eliminating other options, Brenda decided that the only thing she was really interested in was fashion design; yet she knew little about it.

Tapping her personal network first, Brenda called her sister-in-law, a fashion designer who was now a buyer for a major department store. The following week, she returned to the seminar visibly discouraged. Her sister-in-law had told her how competitive the field was and how little chance someone without a bachelor's degree in art had of getting into graduate school. Not one to give up easily, Brenda talked to other designers, but she got the same response. In essence, her contacts were all saying the same thing: "You've got to pay your dues, just like I did."

After some prodding from the group, Brenda went to speak to some students in fashion design at the local university. One of them said that she had been in a similar situation and described a program in Boston that prepares people who did not major in art for careers in design. Participants learn whether they've got the needed talents and develop portfolios for application to graduate school. Apparently, these applications meet with great success, and many students go on to very successful careers. Brenda is now pursuing that program and is hopeful it will lead her away from doing the one thing she hates to do with clothing, sell it.

The lesson of Brenda's story is that you must investigate your intended occupation thoroughly. The more specialized the field you are considering, the more likely you are to encounter people who will discourage you from pursuing it unless you have the same background they have and are willing to travel the same rigorous route they did.

There are many means to any given end. If you really want something, it just may be worth going that extra mile, taking that different route, and charting your own unique course. A good job is worth the struggle. And remember, you only need one.

Old Dogs

Demon 2

You can't teach an old dog new tricks.

Disciple 2

**You're not an old dog,
and you don't need tricks.**

This demon crops up mostly when people shift from one arena to another. These people, concerned that their skills are really not transferable, see themselves as imposters in any world but the one in which they've been. They lack the confidence, not to learn new skills, but to present the skills they have in a way that will be understandable to the people who do the hiring in the new arena.

Tim H.: A Case of Mistaken Identity

Tim H. was a social studies teacher who decided to make a switch to the business world. He knew it was time to get out of teaching when he found he wanted to drop-kick his students rather than educate them. Tim decided he would like to work in corporate training, but his initial efforts to get a job were fruitless. Eventually, he gave up his search, convinced he did not have the skills to be a corporate trainer.

What Tim didn't realize was that he did have the skills but just didn't know how to translate them into the language of corporate trainers. Until he realized that he needed to speak this language, he was doomed to be rejected as just another disgruntled teacher looking for an escape hatch.

After working with Tim for a while, I suggested that he talk with some corporate trainers about what they do and take careful notes after each conversation, paying particular attention to the words they used to describe their responsibilities. After a few conversations, it dawned on him that these people did the same things he did.

Tim approached subsequent interviews using the native tongue. Instead of talking about "curriculum development," he talked about "program design." He referred to his "administrative duties" as his "management experience"; and instead of talking about his "teaching skills," he described his "platform skills." Tim eventually got the job he wanted. In fact, he had to choose from several offers.

Perhaps the most important thing to remember when you shift into a new arena is that you don't need to learn new tricks; you just need to get the attention of—and be willing to become part of—the new pack.

Blowing Your Horn

Demon 3
Don't blow your own horn.

Disciple 3
**You have to blow your own horn;
just be sure to play a melodic tune.**

When presenting themselves for a job, promotion, or transfer, most people make this mistake more often than not. Either they sell themselves short, or they exaggerate their abilities to such a degree that no one would want to work with them.

I recently sat in on two interviews in which the applicant eliminated him/herself by playing too long a tune. In one, the man responded to the request, "Tell us about yourself," with a forty-five-minute, stand-up presentation complete with visual aids. In the other, a woman who was the most qualified applicant on paper eliminated herself by demonstrating her newly learned assertiveness skills in a rather aggressive fashion. It was a shame; she would have done a great job if her prospective colleagues had been willing to work with her.

An even worse liability is the tendency to downplay your abilities in the name of modesty. This quick test will show if you victimize yourself in this way.

	Yes	No
1. When someone congratulates you on a job well done, do you sometimes say, "Oh, it was nothing"?	____	____
2. When describing your skills, do you tend to say, "I *think* I am good at ____," instead of, "I am good at ____"?	____	____
3. When new people enter your organization, do you wait for them to introduce themselves rather than introducing yourself first?	____	____
4. When an opportunity arises to gain some recognition, do you tend to let it go instead of pursuing it?	____	____
5. Do you use phrases such as "pretty sure," "my guess is," and "I imagine" when expressing your opinion?	____	____
6. Does your résumé state the facts, just the facts, and nothing but the facts?	____	____
7. Do you shy away from the idea of having your résumé typeset because you do not want to appear presumptuous?	____	____
8. Does the thought of soliciting a job interview make you queasy?	____	____

	Yes	No
9. Do you feel it is unreasonable to expect an offer of a top salary if you are negotiating a career change?	_____	_____
10. Do you believe that ultimately the most qualified person will get the job?	_____	_____

If you answered yes to at least three of these questions, chances are you are guilty of not blowing your horn enough. You owe it to yourself to be clear about what your strengths are and to make them known to others. That is the only way to get the essential visibility you need to get the jobs you want.

Politics

Demon 4

That new arena is too political.

Disciple 4

**All arenas are political;
what varies are the stakes.**

In his autobiography, *Kissinger, White House Years,* Henry Kissinger talks about the nature of politics. He compares the activities of the State Department to those of a school board. Just as the school board is sometimes stalemated over which company to buy bus tires from, the State Department sometimes gets stuck over which bid to accept on a defense contract. Dr. Kissinger implies that political skills are generic. The vying for position and use of influence that go on in the State Department and on the school board are identical. The only difference (though it is an important one), is that we all have a lot more to lose if the State Department makes a mistake.

Any time you have more than two people—some would argue more than one person—you have a political situation. Also, everyone has a certain range of political skills, a particular way of operating politically. These skills appear at a very early age and develop throughout life.

The other day, my three-year-old son asked me if he could have some ice cream. I said no because he had just eaten a batch of cookies. He then asked my wife, and she said yes. (She didn't know about the cookies.) He got himself a generous portion of ice cream and ate it (out of my range of vision, of course). When I later confronted him with the empty dish, he respectfully told me that "Mommy said I could" and went off to play. The ice cream is inconsequential; the point is that at three, he has already demonstrated two fairly sophisticated political skills: the ability to judge what to tell to whom and the wisdom to cover his actions! I'm confident he will be able to survive in almost any situation by applying his developing resourcefulness.

Limiting yourself because of fear of politics is likely to cost you valuable opportunities that might otherwise offer welcome change. When considering a new situation, don't worry about the politics. If the stakes attract you, pursue them; if they seem too high, pursue them but tread carefully (and see Chapter 5, "Gaining Altitude: Taking Smart Risks").

Serendipity Is No Accident

Demon 5

I'm never lucky when it comes to making changes.

Disciple 5

You can create your own luck.

The dictionary defines *serendipity* as "an aptitude for making desirable discoveries by accident." This definition seems to contradict my contention that serendipity is no accident; in fact, it seems to contradict itself. Is it possible to have an accidental aptitude? What this brings into question is our understanding of such notions as luck, choice, intention, and accident. To manage your career successfully, you have to confront your beliefs about such notions and develop an approach that enhances the likelihood of good fortune coming your way.

My job at the University of Massachusetts is a good example. It's a wonderful job that affords me a reasonable and comfortable life-style, allows me to work with people in a very meaningful and productive way, provides me with a variety of invaluable personal and professional resources, and is largely responsible for my ability to write this book.

But it hasn't always been that way. I started at the university in a much less satisfying role and quit after six weeks (not a strategy I recommend). Because I did not want to leave with a blemish on my record, I requested an exit interview with the director of the unit to explain my actions. I did not know at the time that the second-in-command also suggested that the director and I talk.

We met for lunch and found we had similar views about many of the problems with the job. At the end of the meeting, the director invited me to stay on temporarily as a consultant to pilot a new program. Seven years later, that program forms the basis for this book.

Some would say I was just plain lucky. The director herself often refers to the event as serendipitous. Although it's true that a certain amount of luck was involved, there were a number of intentional factors, some of which I didn't even know about at the time. There was the director's frame of reference; she thought the problems were with the job rather than with me. There was the second-in-command's perspective; he thought I had been handed a difficult situation and let his view be known. Finally, there was my own attitude. When the director suggested I stay on as a consultant, I was reluctant. My early experience had soured me, and I wasn't sure if this was an opportunity or a way to temporarily prolong my dissatisfaction. But I had just decided to marry and thought it would be better to have a job than risk having my wife think I was a worthless hack. More important, it seemed that with all the forces leading me into this situation, I would be a fool to pass it up.

The one element that carried the situation to its positive resolution was that each of us believed things could be worked out and acted accordingly. It is this openness to good fortune, this expectation that things will work out that fosters luck. Openness to positive outcomes creates conditions that will lead other people to look at your career maneuvering and say, "What a lucky person."

Change

Demon 6

**Change is too overwhelming;
I wouldn't know how to go about it.**

Disciple 6

**Use your everyday coping skills,
and approach this problem as
though it were just another work
responsibility.**

There's a movie called *Lovesick* about a psychiatrist who falls in love with one of his patients. Another patient is a street person, a former physics professor who suffers delusions that Martians are electronically "jamming his brain" and scrambling his thoughts. The psychiatrist, after trying more conventional means, offers his patient an aluminum foil hat to block the electronic signals. The patient immediately responds and improves in his day-to-day survival skills.

Over the years, I've met many people in transition who could use that aluminum foil hat. Recent research on neuropsychology suggests that a key difference between healthy

people and dysfunctional people may be that healthy people are able to process and sort out the barrage of thoughts that flood their brains constantly but that dysfunctional people cannot. Although people in the throes of managing career changes are not necessarily dysfunctional, many seem to lose their ability to sort information and perform in the competent way to which they are accustomed.

I suspect their sorting mechanisms become overloaded by too much information and a sense of helplessness arising out of a perceived inability to control events. Because we are led to believe that we receive jobs rather than procure them, it is easy to understand this feeling.

My strategy for conquering this demon is twofold. First, put your foil hat on, and apply all the skills you use in other situations (e.g., problem solving, organizational, interpersonal) to the career management task at hand. Second, remember that nothing perpetuates a feeling of helplessness more than behaving helplessly. Do something, *anything,* to improve your situation, and you'll find yourself building momentum. Summon up your skills and use them. You'll soon find yourself with options that you may have believed were beyond your grasp.

Where to Start

Demon 7
I don't know where to start.

Disciple 7
Start anywhere and everywhere.

When my wife and I decided to have a family a few years ago, we experienced difficulty conceiving a child. Like many of our generation, we had waited until our thirties to have children. After a year of ill-fated efforts, we decided to pursue every avenue we could to achieve results. We took fertility tests, joked about—but carefully read—the book *How to Get Pregnant*, and methodically tried to predict our most fertile times. But more important, we made the search a priority in our lives.

One day, as I was returning from a business trip, I sat next to a man who was reading some complicated looking computer printouts. As I glanced at them—being nosy is sometimes a prerequisite to successful change—I noticed the names of hormones we had recently been dwelling on in our quest for results. I asked him what he was working on, and he told me he was an obstetrician doing research on infertility. The poor man had just done the last bit of reading I would allow him that trip! As a result of our conversation, I learned of a new test being performed on a limited basis in my area that held promise for some cases of infertility. I thanked him for his help and followed the lead. That lead resulted in the conception of our son.

Some will say that this story, too, is one of pure luck, especially those who know our son. However, had I not been focused on the issue, I wouldn't have recognized anything on the printout and would have never asked the doctor about his work. The point is—and I've seen this work countless times—once you really focus on something, the information you need starts to flow in.

Elaine S.: A Meeting at the Bridge

I recently had a client who decided she wanted to be a video technician at a television station, with the hope of eventually moving into production. Because she had no experience, she felt shy about talking to people at stations and was even hesitant to sign up for courses in TV production. During a session in which she felt particularly stuck, we talked about the need to focus her attention on her goal. She reluctantly agreed to make some calls about interviews and classes.

On her way home, she passed a man taking some still photographs of a covered bridge and noticed the call letters of a local TV station on his car. After about a half mile, she turned around and went back to talk with him. It turned out he was taking some shots for a documentary on which he was working. After a forty-five minute conversation, the man offered to let her spend a day with him, carrying equipment and learning more about the business. With his help, she eventually got an entry-level job as a technician and is taking production courses that will equip her to move up in the field. She attributes her success to the meeting at the bridge.

The Universal "They"

Demon 8

"They" (management, the new employer)
will never buy my idea. The system is too
inflexible.

Disciple 8

There is no universal "they" to stop you.
Until you try, you never
know what's possible.

More often than not, people are prevented from carving a niche for themselves by self-imposed constraints. Until you open yourself up to the possibilities, you remain the victim of your environment rather than its architect. Remember:

**Organizations need good people
as much as people need
good organizations.**

My files are full of examples of people who were able to redesign their jobs to match their needs because they were valued organizational members.

Ingrid H.: Sometimes Two Hats Are Better Than One

Ingrid H. was a chief radiology technician at a small private hospital. When the head of the department resigned, Ingrid was asked to take on administrative duties in addition to her technical role, with a substantial pay increase. At first she was delighted, and so was the rest of the staff—one of their own was now in charge. But problems arose. While doing her administrative work, she would frequently be interrupted to take an Xray. While working with patients, she would frequently be interrupted by telephone calls. When I met Ingrid, she was at the end of her rope, ready to quit in spite of the fact that she loved both aspects of her work. After some strategizing, she came to the conclusion that her problem was the structure of her new position. She realized she was constantly being pulled in two equally demanding directions.

Ingrid went back to her supervisor and staff and negotiated the following change: On Monday through Thursday, she would be a technician in full uniform, with no administrative interruptions. On Fridays, she would be strictly an administrator in street clothes and would see no patients. Because her administrative work took about 20 percent of her time and the new arrangement meant that everyone would get her full attention during "their" time, all parties were delighted, especially Ingrid.

Before deciding to leave your job, be sure to explore alternatives within the organization. Many people assume that their current job description is written in stone. If you can make some changes in the structure, duties, or expectations of your role, it can sometimes make the difference (provided you want to stay in the organization) between a minor but significant change and a total redirection.

Time

Demon 9
I don't have the time to make a change.

Disciple 9
This is all the time you have.
Use it to your best advantage.

I've often heard Ken Blanchard, co-author of *The One-Minute Manager* and an expert on the concept of the use of one's time. say, "There will always be sixty seconds in a minute and sixty minutes in an hour, so stop waiting for more time."

I think what he's getting at—and I tend to agree—is that people use the lack of time as an excuse for not doing what is important to them. It is particularly important to come to terms with this excuse in the management of your career. Chances are that you will be managing your job while you make career changes (those of you who are unemployed cannot use this excuse), which gives you the perfect reason—your job—for not taking the time to improve your career. Think about the irony of this for a moment:

**You are too busy doing what you hate
to make time for creating what
you would love.**

I don't want to make this sound simpler than it is. Putting energy into charting a new future while you're working in a draining, dissatisfying job takes a lot of stamina. It also takes organization. There are many books and seminars to help you learn to manage your time. If you need help in this area, use those resources. Most of you, I suspect, are capable of managing your time. What you need is to shift your priorities so that you see your career as the top priority.

**Show me an organization whose top
priority is taking care of its people, and
I'll show you a one-person organization.**

Even the most people-centered organization has a goal beyond its people, and that is the perpetuation of the organization itself. And just as organizations must consider their own interests first in order to survive, people must consider their interests first in order to survive—and thrive.

There are many ways to make your career your first priority. Some people choose one evening a week to work on career activities, others do it on weekends, and others use personal, vacation, or sick time. These are all reasonable approaches (remember, you are as important as your job).

I've seen people shift their duties around to allow them some time to do career-related activities during the workday. If you choose this route, make sure that you're doing an adequate job so that you don't jeopardize your current position. Take care not to do anything illegal or unethical. Just remember:

**The only person who views your career
as top priority is you.**

Fear of the Unknown

Demon 10

**I'm afraid I'll end up liking the new
situation less than the old.**

Disciple 10

**There are many ways to explore
possibilities before making changes.**

This demon preys on its victim's fear of the unknown. I have a friend who is pursued by this demon in his relationships with women. Anxious about starting new relationships, he gets as involved as he can as quickly as possible in order to avoid the unknown. The relationships usually end abruptly and painfully. He is aware that his behavior is self-destructive and likens it to a swimmer diving into a too-shallow pool head first, hitting bottom, and floating to the surface for a slow recovery. Those of you who share his fear of the unknown should consider this:

**For an experienced swimmer, there are
many ways to test the water
before diving in.**

Fred R.: From Computations to Complications

Fred R. was an experienced design engineer who had moved up the ranks to a senior position. His vice president, anxious to keep him happy, decided to promote him to manager of engineering. Fred was pleased with the status and financial benefits of his new role and accepted without hesitation.

The next six months were horrible. Unaccustomed to dealing with "people problems," Fred found his new role extremely frustrating. In his previous position, he had worked on product development and did not have to deal with others very often. Now, placed in charge of the complicated interpersonal dynamics of his staff, Fred felt increasingly incompetent and sank into a deep depression. Realizing he hated his new role, and unwilling to return to his old one because he feared loss of face, he had no alternative but to leave the company and find a new job that was more like his old one.

What happened to Fred has happened to countless other professionals whose paths lead them increasingly away from their preferred work style (in the case of this engineer, methodical) to a less satisfying approach (in Fred's case, highly interactive).

At first glance, the lesson of this story might seem to be: Don't get in over your head. But the real message is: Look before you leap. There are many strategies for getting information (see Occupational Investigation in the POINT Process) before you make a decision. The important thing to remember is that you need not fear the unknown; you just need to make it less mysterious.

Inertia, Laziness, and the Formless Fears

Demon 11
I'm too lazy.

Disciple 11
What's really stopping you?

A Eugene O'Neill play called *The Emperor Jones* tells the story of a man who rises above his humble roots to become emperor of a distant land. One day, he learns that his people are planning to overthrow him. Fearing for his life, he escapes into the forest, where he has a series of imaginary encounters with his past and with some creatures called the "little formless fears" that hover around his feet and confuse his direction. Overcome by his past mistakes and "formless fears," the emperor becomes disoriented and inadvertently backtracks to his original entry point to the forest, where he is taken by his hunters.

Like the Emperor Jones, many people carry with them memories of negative experiences that keep them from doing their best. I recently worked with a woman who had been fired from her teaching job because she was unable to control her classes. The event leading to her dismissal had occurred nine months prior to our meeting, yet she had done little since then to find new work. She often described herself as lazy, unmotivated, and "full of inertia." As we got more into planning for her future, it became evident that this experience was still foremost in her mind and was preventing her from taking any sort of action. In talking further, I discovered she had developed a rather elaborate scenario in her mind wherein her former principal and other colleagues blackballed her in the community, making it impossible for her to find work. Her memory of her failure plus her fantasy of other people's enduring opposition left her unable to act.

Eventually, she met with her former principal, who agreed to write her a letter of recommendation and to help in any way he could. Once this relationship was resolved, the "formless fears" disappeared, her energy increased, and she soon found more suitable work at which she has been very successful.

At the same time I met this woman, I also met a man who was victimized by "formless fears." He was always asking me, "If I do this, what if this happens?" His concerns ranged from what color paper to use for his résumé to what to do if he got a job offer he didn't want. Although he was very active on the phone with me, his motivation went no further. After several weeks of batting around insignificant fears, we had a conversation about his last job. I found out he had been passed over for a promotion in favor of someone his son's age. He was so stunned by this event that he stopped believing in his own marketability. (He was a mechanical engineer with a strong management record, and his fears were truly formless.) Convinced that he was over the hill at forty-five, he developed an image of himself as an aging incompetent. Through a series of conversations and completion of his CareerMap Profile, he managed to change his self-perception from worthless to worthwhile. With some additional help from a therapist along the way, he managed to overcome his inertia and once again find gainful employment.

Events in our lives send us messages about our abilities. When these messages are positive, they fuel us; when they are negative, they slow us down. It is sometimes easy to deal with the negative messages by thinking of yourself as lazy or "unmotivated." When I was training to be a counselor, a professor gave me what has proven to be a good piece of advice: "Never trust the word *lazy*. There's usually something more concrete going on underneath. Find out what that is, work on that, and the laziness problem will go away."

It is easy to avoid coming to terms with negative feelings by blaming laziness or inertia or by dwelling on formless fears. When you find yourself falling prey to the potential dangers of the forest, remember the words of the Emperor Jones:

Ain't nothin' there but the trees.

Wanting to Change

Demon 12

**Wanting to change is childish,
irresponsible, and a sign of immaturity.**

Disciple 12

**Wanting to change is natural, normal,
predictable, and grown-up.**

One of the best results of my career seminars occurs at the beginning, when people realize that the other participants are not losers. Seeing people from all walks of life, of all ages, and at all income levels who admit they don't know what to do next provides a jolt of energy and a feeling of relief that the best motivational speaker could not equal.

**The biggest myth about midlife
crisis is that it happens only at midlife.**

This chapter is about to end where it began. Change is inevitable. Researchers have spent years trying to categorize the developmental stages people go through, and many of you have read the popularized versions of this research. Although there is debate among experts about what happens when, there is little doubt that if the desire, the often compelling need, to create change in one's work is left unaddressed, it can lead to inordinate stress. In other words:

**Career longevity may be
hazardous to your health.**

If you are one of those rare people who has found a life's work that is truly satisfying and offers you the variety, stimulation, and ability to grow that every person needs, this statement may not apply to you. But if you're like most of us, you need to realize and accept that significant change in the way you spend your time is inevitable and critical to your well-being. You also need to realize that you are unique and that only *you* know what sort of changes you need. Whether you're twenty-five or eighty-five or somewhere in between, your mind needs to be exercised, and your spirit needs to be enlivened if you are to remain healthy. So the next time someone reacts negatively to your desire to change, or you reprimand yourself for it, remember:

**The drive to change is not frivolous;
it's imperative.**

FIVE

Gaining Altitude: Taking Smart Risks

The Nature of Career Risk Taking

**A good risk is one that is
likely to end in success.**

NOBODY LIKES to lose, but for some, the fear of losing is so great that they never venture forth at all. For others, the thrill that accompanies a risk is so intoxicating that they welcome every opportunity to take a chance. Most people at one time or another have found themselves wishing that they had been a little more daring or played it a little safer. Ideally, everyone should develop the ability to assess a risk and determine how much daring and how much safety are appropriate. This chapter presents a model for managing the risk-taking process.

Adele S.: From the Frying Pan to the Fire

Adele S. is one of the most courageous people I know. When I met her, she was working as a marketing manager for a commodities brokerage firm in New England. Her job was very demanding, involving long hours and constant stress. Satisfied with her financial package, working environment, and life-style, Adele was somewhat puzzled by her emerging discontent. As I got to know her, I learned that she had entered marketing through her graphic design work and that she was a talented painter. I knew we were making progress when she became teary-eyed each time we talked about her artwork. After several weeks, it became clear that although she loved the pace, variety, and financial rewards of her job, she was not interested in the commodities market. Spending her time helping other people make money just didn't turn her on. Her real desire was to work in the art world.

Unwilling to give up the financial rewards and stimulation of her job, Adele faced a real dilemma. Although shifting her focus to her painting would have taken care of her artistic needs, she would have to give up too much. She had no desire, as she put it, "to become like one of my starving artist friends."

I was surprised when Adele came into my office to tell me she was selling her house in the Berkshires and moving to New York City. She had decided that the only place she could get the stimulation and focus on art she wanted and still make a lot of money was in a large city, most likely New York. Her plan was to stay with a friend in the city and look for work as an account manager or broker for a firm dealing in high-priced art. After strategizing a bit, Adele decided to minimize the risk somewhat and rent her house for a year in case she decided to return. She never did return, and after a few "bridge-building" jobs, she landed a very lucrative position as a manager of a prestigious corporate art collection.

Adele's risk-taking style was striking because of her willingness to establish priorities and make risk-related decisions based on those priorities and her ability to soften the risk by making it less irreversible (i.e., holding onto her house for an interim period).

Risk for the Sake of Risk

You all know people whose risk-related behavior seems less balanced than Adele's. One of the most notorious in recent years was presidential candidate Gary Hart. Shortly before his apparent tryst with model Donna Rice, Hart dared reporters—who were already suspicious about his marital fidelity—to follow him around. He then allowed himself to be photographed with his secret companion and chose a yacht named *Monkey Business* for his trip to Bimini. Viewing the situation from a risk-taking perspective, one could easily conclude that Hart's greatest fault was not his lust for women but his lust for the thrill of the gamble. His re-entry into the race after what most observers agreed was too short a hiatus is yet another sign of his affinity for risk.

Many people suffer from a need for the stimulation that accompanies daring adventures. For them, the challenge in career risk taking is to control that need and create strategies that enhance their stability. At the other end of the spectrum are people who fear risk so much that they hang onto whatever they've got even if they hate it. These are the people who don't buy a lottery ticket even though they would like to because they don't want to risk losing a dollar. They're the same people who, at the beginning of their careers, base their decisions about whether or not to stay in a job on the organization's retirement plan.

The alternative is to develop a risk-taking style that is neither cavalier nor paranoid, one that takes into consideration all the relevant factors and makes the most of the risk. To grasp the complexity of effective risk taking, one needs to understand what people who succeed in their risks do to balance the scales in their favor.

Mastering Risk: A Tale of Two Risk Takers

Don K.

Don K. was a successful marketing manager for a large building supply company. At forty-one, he was well paid and loved traveling to meet with his national network of clients. His goal was to move from manufacturing to education by age forty-five, but he found it difficult to give all this up for the modest life of the classroom. However, he still felt driven by his interest in education and wanted to shift from providing products to providing learning experiences. Giving up marketing for teaching felt like too great a risk, but he found an alternative that, although still risky, offered him the best of both worlds.

Don bought a marketing training franchise that specializes in providing training to sales personnel. He is targeting the sales forces of building supply companies and launching his business by tapping his formidable network of contacts. He will continue traveling and will spend one-third of his time conducting the training, which will fulfill his desire to educate others.

Barbara W.

Barbara W. is a hairdresser who spent twelve years cutting hair in other people's shops. She came to see me with two concerns: She was tired of working for other people, and she craved greater meaning in her work. One of the things I noticed quickly about Barbara was that she had an ability to make others feel comfortable. Also, she was quite knowledgeable about skin care, as well as hair care.

Eventually, she decided on a path that addressed both her need for autonomy and her need for meaningful work—and one that was likely to succeed. She opened her own hair salon and began studying the field of cosmetic alternatives for restorative plastic surgery patients. Working with people who have specialized cosmetic needs has provided her with meaningful work that utilizes her interpersonal skills, and her haircutting business provides her with the bulk of her income. She has established relationships with several surgeons in the area and hopes to eventually do more recovery work and less salon work.

The interesting thing about Barbara and those like her is that they seem to be able to apply their risk-taking skills to a variety of life situations. The other day, Barbara told me a story that illustrates this point. Barbara is in her late thirties, single, and interested in meeting new men. Frustrated with the conventional approaches, she considered responding to a personal ad. Her friends cautioned her against it, and she was concerned about going on a date with a stranger and ending up in an uncomfortable situation. Eventually, however, she responded to a particular ad and suggested a meeting at a restaurant for lunch, an arrangement that considerably reduced the amount of risk. The meeting didn't pan out, but Barbara feels she has uncovered a low-risk, comfortable way to meet new men and is happy with the balanced approach she has created.

Becoming a Renaissance Risk Taker

Both Don and Barbara are what I call *Renaissance risk takers*. Although they risk a great deal, they compromise none of their most valued priorities.

Earlier, I talked about two types of risk takers: those who risk too much and those who don't risk enough. This section is designed to encourage you to become (or to continue to be) a Renaissance risk taker. Like the Renaissance man of literary lore, the Renaissance risk taker operates by "encompassing the full spectrum of available knowledge."*

In the case of risk taking, "the full spectrum of available knowledge" refers to a depth of understanding of the intricacies of a particular risk, with emphasis on using this knowledge to tilt the scales in one's favor. A Renaissance risk taker risks neither too much nor too little. By learning to balance potential losses and potential gains, he/she learns to choose risks that are likely to end in success.

The way to be a Renaissance risk taker is to become adept at understanding the various aspects of a given risk and at choosing the right risks and carrying them through. This process and the knowledge and skill needed for it are fostered through the use of the Risk Assessment Process.

Before moving to the Risk Assessment Process, I'd like to point out one aspect of risk taking that seems critical to success: the ability to tolerate ambiguity. Many people on the edge of a risky venture wait until they have a reasonable assurance that they will be successful. Unfortunately, the nature of risk taking precludes such conditions.

There is no such thing as a sure risk.

Random House College Dictionary, revised edition, 1975.

But although it is not possible to ensure a positive outcome, there are ways to minimize negative results and to strategize for survival if the risk backfires. Both are important skills in the Renaissance risk taker's repertoire. So before risking, you need to consider: (1) your ability to tolerate the inevitable ambiguity, (2) what you might do to minimize the potential negative outcomes, and (3) what you might do if things don't work out.

**Never risk more than
you're willing to lose.**

Renaissance risk taking involves assessing a risk, making decisions based on a full understanding of the parameters of that risk, and being aware of the possibilities and alternative actions you can take to ensure results that you, at best, feel overjoyed with and, at least, can live with.

The Risk Assessment Process

This seven-step process will improve your ability to make sound judgments about career-related risks. I have used and refined this process over the years, and it has proved to be an effective tool for helping people weigh the various aspects of a career risk and choose appropriate action. I have seen people use it to help with such "minor" things as rearranging their schedule to such major things as submitting a resignation.

The best way for you to test this process is to identify a real risk you are currently considering; using a hypothetical situation will yield hypothetical results. Should you decide to risk venturing through this process (the mere thought of it scares some people), you will find yourself with a concrete plan for moving forward.

For each step, I will give you brief instructions, ask you to do some writing, and then discuss key aspects of that particular step. Good luck.

Step 1

Identify the risk, and be as specific as possible. Pick a risk that you haven't yet taken but would consider taking. Don't choose something that scares the daylights out of you, but don't pick something that feels like no big deal, either. Try to choose a situation that has a moderate sense of risk attached to it.

Examples: asking for a raise, renegotiating responsibilities, saying no to a promotion, transferring to another department, talking to a headhunter.

Describe the action you are considering:

_____

_____

_____

_____

_____

Congratulations! You've just taken that all-important first step of articulating, in writing, a risky situation that you're not sure how to act on. If you're one of the overcautious risk takers, you may be feeling nervous, but you have acknowledged your willingness to *consider* acting. If you're one of the overindulgent risk takers, you've made the first move toward changing your pattern and taking more calculated risks.

If you haven't been able to write anything, you may want to examine what it is that is stopping you from experimenting with this process. Think about your own demons and disciples, and force yourself to commit yourself on paper to fine-tuning your risk-related behavior.

Step 2

Unless you risk exclusively for the thrill of risking, the move you are considering has some positive potential outcomes for you. In this step, you will consider all the benefits that might come of taking this risk, including psychological, emotional, intellectual, social, political, physical, financial, and spiritual gains.

List all the possible gains that come to mind if you decide to take this risk.

_____

_____

_____

_____

_____

Step 3

Now that you've identified what you have to gain, you may be raring to go. Unfortunately, real risk is not quite that simple. Before making the ultimate decision on whether to act, you need to look at what you have to lose. If you can't think of anything you could lose, the move you're considering is not serious enough to be called a risk because inherent in any risk is the potential for loss. What you need to do now is bring that potential loss into focus. Consider what you have to lose in the realms of the psychological, emotional, intellectual, social, political, physical, financial, and spiritual.

   List the possible losses that come to mind if you decide to take this risk.

_____

_____

_____

_____

_____

Step 4

You have just focused on one of the most debilitating forces related to taking risks: the fear of loss. The interesting thing is that for any given risk, each person's list of potential losses and the relative weight of those losses are different. This next step involves focusing on those losses that seem to be the worst and coming up with ways to minimize them before you take the risk. (Adele's hanging onto her house, Don's sticking with familiar clientele for his new business, and Barbara's continuing to cut hair while developing her cosmetology skills are all examples of how successful risk takers minimize the potential negative outcomes of their actions.) To minimize your potential negative outcomes, choose the three worst-possible losses, and strategize about how you might minimize their impact.

List the three potential losses and your strategies for lessening their consequences.

1. _____

_____

_____

2. _____

_____

_____

3. _____

_____

_____

If you couldn't come up with ways to minimize your three strongest negative outcomes, this risk may not be a wise one for you to take. You may be considering risking more than you're willing to lose.

The other possibility is that you're grappling with a situation that scares you in a way that is preventing you from using the adaptive resources and coping skills that normally propel you through difficult situations.

Many people make the mistake of thinking that the level of risk involved in their lives has nothing to do with them and everything to do with the situation. In truth, the extent to which you risk successfully is related to the extent to which you can frame that risk in terms that make sense to you, thereby increasing your likelihood of survival and success. An example is the best way to illustrate this point.

Denny W.: Anatomy of a Risk Taker

Denny W. was the managing editor of a medium-sized newspaper. One of the first things he said when we met was, "I've been carried out of the newsroom on a stretcher twice, and I don't want to die there." Denny is an interesting guy who, when he's not writing editorials lambasting the local union, is either white-water kayaking or mountain climbing. He once spent nine days in a tent under an avalanche not knowing whether he'd survive. He's not someone you would think of as an overanxious risk taker. However, after completing his CareerMap Profile, he said, "Now *this* is terrifying." He was referring to the prospect of giving up newspaper work and moving to another part of the country. (He was born about 200 yards from where he worked.) The thought of uprooting himself and giving up the only work he had ever known made white water rapids and tumbling mountains of snow seem like child's play.

Denny's fear of changing blinded him to the fact that he had all the resources he needed for making the kinds of changes he was considering. The blinders came off when one of his friends, in disbelief that he could be scared of anything, suggested he think about his potential career shift as a mountain climb. He likened the research he would do in pursuit of new work to swinging off the side of a mountain without knowing what was around the next corner but remaining anchored to the mountain for protection. When Denny looked at his risk in these terms, it seemed much less frightening, and he was able to move carefully and methodically in his chosen direction.

Step 5

Now that you've assessed the potential damage associated with your risk and the potential gains, you've decided either that it's too dangerous or that it might be worth pursuing. If you've abandoned this risk, go back to step 1, identify another risk that seems worth considering, and repeat the process. If you're still in gear (i.e., if you have minimized the negatives to the point where taking the risk still seems reasonable), it is time to summon the courage, skills, and insight to move forward. Just as Denny realized that moving was no more demanding than mountain climbing and that changing jobs was no more complicated than running a newsroom, you need to find personal metaphors that support your capacity to take this risk. In other words, what evidence is there in your life that suggests you are capable of taking this risk and succeeding? For this activity, you may want to refer back to the list of achievements you completed in Chapter 2 (page 36). As you review that list or think about past successes, do you find any experiences that would suggest you are capable of doing what you are thinking about doing?

List past experiences that at least hint at or at best emphasize your ability to succeed in your proposed venture. Search for at least three events that in some way suggest you might be able to handle this risk.

_____

_____

_____

_____

_____

If you came up with three or more pieces of evidence and you've gotten this far, you're probably on your way to taking the plunge. If you couldn't find any evidence of past successes that in some way reflect your potential to pull off this risk, make sure you've done a thorough search. If you still come up dry, take a look at the risk, and see if you've been too ambitious in your initial planning. If you have, you may want to modify your idea and start the process again.

Step 6

Now that you've assessed what you have to lose and gain, have minimized the potential losses, begun to overcome your fears, and determined that you indeed have what it takes to pull off this risk, there's one more thing to consider before moving into action. It would be nice to think that with the right preparation, any risk you take will be successful. Unfortunately, there are a myriad of unforeseen forces operating outside your control that can affect your success. For example, a woman I know of left her job, planning to take a year off to explore options. She had invested in the stock market successfully and planned to live for that year on her dividends. She left her office on October 19, 1987, only to find that the stock market crash had left her with only 40 percent of her planned income. Surely she could not have foreseen that. Fortunately, she did have an alternative plan and was able to secure work until she could regroup and try again.

Although there is a certain measure of risk required for any success, having a fallback plan can make the difference between surviving a defeat and being crushed by it. Having such a plan also frees you from worry about survival and optimizes your ability to act creatively. Before you move ahead with any substantial risk, make sure you position yourself to survive if things don't work out.

Write down your strategy for survival and recovery if the risk doesn't work out. Include a plan of action that would cut your losses and lead you to developing a new strategy.

_____

_____

_____

_____

_____

This step is critical, particularly for those of you who fit the profile of the careless risk taker. As I've mentioned throughout this chapter, a good risk is one that is likely to end in success, but that doesn't mean it will. I strongly believe that you should risk as often and as wisely as you can to move toward what you really want but that you should also do all you can to prevent your own disasters.

Step 7

Now that you've made it through the obstacle course, you're ready to take action. If you've worked through the first six steps of this process carefully, there's a good chance that you're in position to go for it. This final step is simple.

Outline the actions you need to take to initiate this risk.

Action 1 _____

_____

Action 2 _____

_____

Action 3 _____

_____

Action 4 _____

_____

Action 5 _____

_____

You have now completed the risk-assessment process. But before you move on to the "taking action" part of this book, I'd like to share one more idea about risk taking.

The Structured and Fluid Nature of Risk Taking

As I've said, I spend a lot of time watching people create changes in their lives and trying to figure out the difference between those who succeed and those who don't. Much of this difference is still a mystery to me, but there are a couple of factors related to risk taking that seem fairly developed in most successful risk takers.

The first is structure: the ability to organize the variables involved in a risk and play out the steps in an orderly fashion. The second is fluidity: the ability to hang loose during a risk-taking process and tolerate the ambiguity that comes with it. The reason many people get stuck when it comes to risk is that most people are good at one or the other, but not both. Either they have a knack for controlling events, or they have an ability to go with the flow. People who are tight organizers yet are simultaneously able to hang loose seem to make the best risk takers.

If you think about it in visual terms for a moment, you can place most people's approach on a continuum from structured to fluid.

Structured ─────────────────────────────── **Fluid**

Where would you place yourself on this continuum? (Mark that spot with an X.)

Now, if you look at successful risk takers, you'll find that they transform this figure. The people I know who are masterful at taking risks bring both their ability to organize and their ability to tolerate ambiguity together so that it looks more like a circle than a continuum.

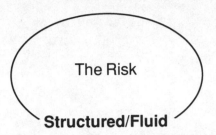

The Risk

Structured/Fluid

This structured yet fluid orientation encompasses the risk. In doing so, it focuses attention on the necessary intricacies inherent in any risky venture while supporting the necessary tolerance of uncertainty that is also inherent.

So if you want to maintain your ability to manage risk and also want to enhance your chances of success, remember:

**Pay close attention to what needs
to be done, and expect and embrace
the unexpected.**

SIX

Navigating Your Course: The POINT Process

A WOMAN walked into my office the other day and told me she had decided to give up her teaching job and become a technical writer. She said that in spite of the fact that there were a lot of jobs around (she lives in an area with a high demand for such writers), she seemed unable to locate them. When I asked who she had talked to so far, she leaned over and said softly, "No one yet. I don't want my principal to find out."

> **Successful people don't hide their plans;**
> **they broadcast them**
> **(at the right time and the right place).**

This chapter is about preparing for and managing successful transitions. Through the POINT Process, you will learn techniques for optimizing your transitions and for creating the conditions likely to lead to a constant flow of increased opportunity.

The POINT Process is:

Persuasive paper work
Occupational investigation
Influential interviewing
Networking
Tracking leads

"P": PERSUASIVE PAPER WORK

Perhaps the most unexciting aspect of career management is the paper work. Because of its uninspiring nature, it is also the most neglected.

> **If I had a dollar for every person I know**
> **who missed a job opportunity because**
> **they didn't have an up-to-date résumé,**
> **I'd be a rich man.**

The secret of creating good paper work is to make it as simple as possible. This section will focus on designing career-related paper work that is persuasive yet simple to produce. Using these techniques will put your chances above those of the vast majority of people who treat such things casually.

From time to time, I ask some of my organizational clients if I can look at résumés in their personnel files. I am continually astonished by the shoddy paper work masquerading as job applications. The files are full of poorly typed, excessively verbose, incredibly boring narratives. A woman recently asked me, "How good does it have to look?"

**It needs to look as good as it
possibly can.**

Your paper work is one of the few aspects of your career over which you have total control. Why not capitalize on this and begin your search ahead of the pack?

First and foremost keep in mind that career-related paper work is sales copy and needs to be prepared like sales copy. You are the product, and your paper work is the advertising.

Résumés

**If you want the résumé done right,
do it yourself.**

I've never understood the professional résumé-writing business. Even if you're a poor writer, you can get a little help from someone with good writing skills and create a résumé that highlights your uniquely marketable talents and reflects who you are. When you have someone else do it for you, the chances of their highlighting your unique abilities are low. It's more likely that they'll make you look like everybody else with a similar background or, worse, like someone you're not or, worse yet, like such an egotist that no one will even want to talk with you. I recently saw an ad that vividly brings this point across:

We Mass Produce Unique Résumés!

Although you want to sell the best "you" possible, you do want to sell *you*, not some high-priced writer's image of you. As my final plea for writing your own résumé, consider this:

**Not writing your own résumé
is like not planning your own wedding.**

I find wedding-planning services as absurd as résumé-writing services. The wedding you choose to have, like the résumé you choose to write, is a reflection of who you are. If you want things to go a certain way, you have to be in control of the action. If all this still hasn't convinced you, think of all the money you'll save producing your own top-quality product rather than paying for a second-rate one.

You are the person best qualified to write your résumé. You are capable of doing it, and you can do the best job. Most important, when your résumé has done its job and gotten you the interview, you'll have the confidence of knowing they are interested in the person who is really behind the piece of paper.

How to Do It

Step 1: What Are You Selling?

The first thing you need to do is decide what aspects of your background are the most compelling: your current and previous jobs, your skills, your accomplishments, your knowledge areas, or your education. Quickly rank the following items from 1 (most impressive) to 6 (least impressive):

_____ Current position
_____ Previous positions
_____ Skills
_____ Accomplishments
_____ Knowledge areas
_____ Education

Step 2: Whom Are You Selling To?

Check the appropriate box.

_____ Someone in your current field
_____ Someone in a new field
_____ Not sure

If you checked the first box, you're ready to move on. If you checked the second box, you need to do some homework (see Demon 2 in Chapter 4, page 78). Learn the language of that new field so that you can speak to them in their own terms. If you're not sure whom you're selling to, you need to backtrack to "Taking Stock" (page 5).

**If you don't know who's buying,
chances are you won't be selling.**

Step 3: What's the Best Way to Present Your Material?

Once you know what you're presenting and whom you're presenting it to, you need to organize your material. In most cases, this material can be organized into four or five categories. Here are some suggestions:

Skill areas	Education
Knowledge areas	Employment history
Areas of expertise	Professional experience
Accomplishments	Observations of superiors
Personal data	Awards/distinctions

Choose the four or five categories (these or other, more appropriate ones) that best match your history and the emphasis of your search. A rule of thumb: If you're staying in the same general field, emphasize work experience and employment history; if you're changing fields, emphasize skills, knowledge, and areas of expertise. (Whatever you do, include work history somewhere.)

There are many acceptable résumé formats. The important thing is to choose the one that best matches you, that accommodates your particular history and highlights what you most want to emphasize. Over the years, I have worked with a couple of models that work well for most people. If they seem to fit your background and aspirations, feel free to use them. However, this book is not intended to be a comprehensive résumé guide. If neither model suits you, there are many good books out there to help you find the right match.

Possible Format for **Changing Fields**

Chris Simpson
42 Porter Street
Philadelphia, PA 01617
(817) 966-0873

Objective: Seeking human resource position in high-technology industry that will utilize my skills in project management, problem solving, and personnel management to improve employee productivity.

AREAS OF EXPERTISE

Project Management

Successfully managed the transition of company accounting system from manual, file-based system to computerized database system. Managed every aspect of the transition, including capital equipment acquisition and installation, personnel training, and integration of new system with other operating systems.

Coordinated the expansion of division's product line to include specialized paper products. Coordinated the implementation of new line, including acquisition of equipment, hiring of personnel, marketing of product, and distribution of first product run.

Problem Solving

Monitored, identified, and resolved problems related to procedures in the technical and human resource areas. Assessed nature of problems, pinpointed requirements for resolution, and implemented problem-solving strategies. Results included consistent maintenance of high product output during transition periods.

Acted as troubleshooter for company when product output in a particular plant was low. In a short period, assessed the problem, made recommendations to management, and supervised activities for resolution of the problem.

Personnel Management

Involved in the hiring and supervision of departmental personnel, including screening applications, conducting interviews, providing orientation, and monitoring employee progress. Responsible for conducting annual performance reviews and making promotion recommendations. Also involved in termination process when necessary.

Developed new positions and position descriptions for personnel as required during company expansion in the areas of accounting, manufacturing, and marketing.

Technical

Use and application of basic accounting principles, including the use of spreadsheets and the creation and analysis of budgets.

Understanding of legal and procedural aspects of personnel policy.

Experience in and knowledge of plant expansion and modification, including various aspects of technical and human resource transitions.

In-depth knowledge of the paper industry.

EMPLOYMENT HISTORY

Team Manager, Continental Paper Company, Philadelphia, PA, 1984-1988.

Assistant Manager of Manufacturing, C.S. Todd Paper Company, Hoboken, NJ, 1980-1984.

Personnel Manager, Seymour Paper Products Co., Newark, NJ, 1977-1980.

EDUCATION

Bachelor of Business Administration, Rutgers University, 1976.

Possible Format for *Staying in Current Field*

Chris Simpson
42 Porter Street
Philadelphia, PA 01617
(817) 966-0873

Objective: Seeking management position in paper products company with substantial responsibility utilizing my expertise in product development, facilities management, and personnel relations.

AREAS OF EXPERTISE

Product Development   Personnel Relations
Project Management   Problem Solving
Facilities Management   Basic Accounting

PROFESSIONAL EXPERIENCE

Team Manager, Continental Paper Company, Philadelphia, PA, 1984-1988.

Responsible for the production output of a twenty-person production team, including supervision of team members, monitoring of production output, troubleshooting equipment problems. Team consistently maintained above-average product output and low employee turnover.

Coordinated the expansion of the division's product line to include specialized paper products. Orchestrated the implementation of the new line, including acquisition of equipment, marketing of product, and distribution of first product run.

Involved in the screening and hiring of employees for own team and other company teams. Developed new position descriptions in cooperation with the personnel department.

Assistant Manager of Manufacturing, C.S. Todd Paper Company, Hoboken, NJ, 1980-1984.

Supervised all production activities of manufacturing group, including monitoring of production output, equipment purchasing and maintenance, employee performance, and quality control.

At request of company president, took on additional responsibility involving the transition of the company accounting system from manual, file-based system to computerized database system. Managed every aspect of the transition, including capital equipment acquisition and installation, personnel training, and integration of new system with other operating systems.

Personnel Manager, Seymour Paper Products Co., Newark, NJ, 1977-1980.

Responsible for the formation and administration of all personnel policies for the company. Developed and maintained system for salary administration and monitoring of benefit packages.

Worked with various department managers to develop job descriptions. Involved in screening and hiring applicants and in orchestrating the termination process when necessary.

EDUCATION

Bachelor of Business Administration, Rutgers University, 1976.

_____

Once you've chosen your format, it's time to plug in your information. To do this, you first need to compose short, direct paragraphs that describe particular aspects of your background. These paragraphs are the heart of your résumé and therefore need the most care. The résumés of Chris Simpson provided some examples. Here are some additional sample paragraphs for the various sections:

SKILL AREAS (Use this when you want to emphasize what you can do based on what you have done.)

Fiscal Management

Experienced in all aspects of fiscal management, including budget preparation, cost analysis, payroll administration, deficit control, and financial planning.

Training

Have designed and conducted training on a broad range of topics for employees at various levels. Experienced in the entire training process, including formulation of goals and objectives, design of lectures and learning activities, presentation of units, and evaluation of participant learning.

KNOWLEDGE AREAS (Use this when you want to emphasize subject matter in which you are expert or of which you have a significant grasp.)

Investment Options

Have a comprehensive understanding of investment options, including stocks, commodities, retirement packages, group investment programs, precious metals, and real estate.

Pharmacology

Have complete knowledge of the properties of drugs related to medicinal use, including the reactions and properties of the various drug groups. Have maintained an up-to-date knowledge of emerging experimental products for use against major diseases.

AREAS OF EXPERTISE (Use this when you want to emphasize a competency for which you have both significant knowledge and skill.)

Insurance Underwriting

Experienced and knowledgeable in all aspects of insurance underwriting, including guidelines for issuing of policies, regulations on limitations of policies, cost distribution, exclusions, risk analysis, and policy preparation.

Computer Systems Analysis

Familiar with all major computer systems used in this country. Experienced with the setting up and debugging of multiunit mainframe computer networks. Specialize in integrating present systems with new technologies.

ACCOMPLISHMENTS (Use this when you want to emphasize experience that demonstrates what you are capable of doing. You can present this material as a separate section or incorporate it at the end of other sections.)

Production Improvement

After examination of production process, modified procedure resulting in the elimination of 20 percent of product defects while speeding up production by 5 percent.

Promotion Campaign

Developed and implemented a promotion campaign for a bank branch with a low number of new customers. Result of campaign was 5 percent quarterly increase in new customers.

PERSONAL DATA (Use this when you have significant non-work experience to convey and have the room for it.)

Fund Raising

Active in the annual fund raising for a community organization providing assistance to the homeless.

Team Management

Managed three sports teams during three different seasons for local school system.

EDUCATION (This information should appear somewhere in the résumé; the placement depends on its relationship to the work sought.)

Standard (Use this format for a traditional educational background.)

M.B.A., Sloan School of Management, Massachusetts Institute of Technology, Cambridge, MA, 1975.

B.A., History, Boston University, Boston, MA, 1974.

NonStandard (Use this format for an unusual or nontraditional educational background.)

B.A., with independent concentration in Economics, University without Walls, Syracuse University, Syracuse, NY, 1984.

Additional Education: six courses taken toward **Masters in Management**; ten seminars in **management and supervision** attended.

EMPLOYMENT HISTORY (Use this when you are changing fields or positions, have elaborated on your abilities elsewhere, and want to provide a simple chronology of employment.)

Vice Principal, Harding Junior High School, Harding, NY, 1983-1988.

Guidance Counselor, Harding Junior High School, Harding, NY, 1978-1982.

Elementary School Teacher, grades five and six, Elm Street School, Harding, NY, 1975-1977.

PROFESSIONAL EXPERIENCE (Use this when you are staying in the same field and wish to describe your experience in the context of your current profession.)

Vice Principal, Harding Junior High School, Harding, NY, 1983-1988.

Administrative responsibilities include initial screening and interviewing of new teachers and staff, the completion of regular demographic reports on the student population, and monitoring of student progress in relation to national standardized tests.

As head disciplinary figure, responsibilities include the development and implementation of strategies for handling student misbehavior, including the creation and monitoring of appropriate disciplinary activities and the establishment and maintenance of individual disciplinary programs for problem students.

Also responsible for the day-to-day operations of the

school, including assuring teacher coverage in all classes, maintaining smooth flow of daily activities, and coordinating activities related to building maintenance and repair.

OBSERVATIONS OF SUPERIORS (Use this when you have references or evaluations that highlight your unique capacity to make a contribution. You can put this information either at the end of another section or as a separate section.)

Example: "At a time when the company was experiencing major problems with its product line, Ms. Johnson demonstrated an uncanny ability to resolve customer complaints." S. Hawthorne, Vice President for Marketing, Humboldt Company.

Example: "During his employment with our company, Mr. Raymond demonstrated a superior ability to uncover and solve technical problems in record time." L. Hutchinson, Manager of Operations, Tennison Computer Company.

AWARDS/DISTINCTIONS (Use this when mention of an award or distinction supports attainment of the employment desired and illustrates your expertise in a relevant area.)

Example: Received "best sales record" award three years in a row.

Once you've created your format and written your paragraphs, you're ready to put them together into coherent form. Here are ten tips that will help you to proceed.

Ten Tips for a Better Résumé

These guidelines can help you to improve your résumé or to design one if you don't already have one. Remember, having a good, updated résumé at all times makes it easier to respond to and apply for possible jobs.

1. Be Thorough

A résumé should describe what you are capable of doing based on what you have done and should include such things as skills, work experience, education, volunteer experience, special achievements, and interesting personal data.

2. Be Creative

Most people use standard résumé forms even if those forms don't fit their particular situation. Don't be afraid to try something a little different; choose your own order of information. For example, if your work experience is more impressive than your education, put it first. Don't be afraid to juggle sections; move them around to suit your own needs.

3. Use Quotes to Emphasize Your Strengths

This is a nice touch when done well. A good place to find usable quotes is in old evaluations or reference letters. Here is an example from a middle manager's annual performance review. "Mr. Ross has demonstrated a high level of skill in organization, resource management, and fiscal accountability during the course of this project." Frank Morgan, Vice President for Marketing, National Convection Company, Scottsdale, AZ.

4. Make It Easy to Read

Many people make the mistake of trying to fit too much information in too little space. A good length for a résumé is one to three pages, but descriptive paragraphs should be short, concise, and to the point.

5. Include a Job Objective If You Have a Clear One

A good objective states what skills you have and would like to use, in what type of setting, and for what purpose. If you don't really know, it's better to leave it out and address the subject in individual cover letters. An objective that is too broad is worse than no objective at all.

6. Be Persuasive About Your Assets

People tend to be too modest when describing their achievements. Although you need to be careful not to go overboard, you must also accent your most appealing traits. Emphasize those things you did well and are proud of.

7. Be Honest

There has been a great deal of publicity in the past few years about people falsifying their credentials. As a result, employers are now checking more carefully for false information. Besides, if you've lied on your résumé, you'll be more nervous in the interview and may run into trouble on the job.

8. Be Specific

Employers are interested in the bottom line. If you say you have budgeting experience explain how large the budget was. The more specific you can be, the better sense the employer will get of what you've done successfully.

9. Spread the Word

Show your résumé to everyone you know. Seek opinions. Make changes. You know you have a good résumé when you no longer feel squeamish about showing it to people.

10. Make It Attractive

Some people think this is silly, but if you're an employer sorting through a stack of résumés, it's easier to pay attention to the ones that are printed clearly on good paper.

Résumés and Personal Style: A Word Before You Get Started

If you still find yourself hesitant to complete this crucial task, you may want to motivate yourself by considering it from the perspective of your preferred work style. If you don't recall (or haven't yet found out) what your preferred style is, refer back to the preferred work style exercise in Chapter 2, page 24.

Once you know what your preferred style is, imagine the task of writing your résumé accordingly:

Creative: Approach your résumé as though it were an empty canvas or an unwritten book.

Methodical: Approach your résumé as though it were a spreadsheet or an elaborate formula.

Practical: Approach your résumé as though it were an instruction manual—user-friendly, of course.

Interactive: Approach your résumé as though it were a letter to an old friend written to convey something very important.

The Ancient Art of Letter Writing

I recently read that the Smithsonian Institution is looking for a personal letter to put in the archives. They are becoming that rare! With competitive telephone rates and the advent of computer networks, writing personal letters is increasingly becoming a lost art. Today, many people are unable to compose a lucid letter. Although business letters and personal letters are obviously quite different, the lack of practice with, and appreciation for, personal letters have stunted the ability to write a letter that has impact. The truth is:

Most people write lousy letters.

Cover Letters

A man walked into my office and challenged me to tell him what was wrong with his cover letters. He had a pile of forty. He said he knew they were well written and portrayed him accurately, yet he had not gotten a single response. A quick glance at them showed me his problem. Although his letters were indeed well written, they were no better than most others I've seen. Each letter announced his interest in the position and then went on to elaborate on his qualifications. His letters reflected a common mistake made by job seekers: the notion that the people reading his letters would find them fascinating. Remember:

**The only person enamored of you
is you.**

People are not going to be compelled to interview you because you say nice things about yourself in your cover letters. What will compel them to interview you is the possibility that you may be a solution to one or more of their problems. A cover letter is an opportunity, albeit a limited one, to whet someone's appetite. Along with a tight, distinctive résumé, it can make the difference between being seen or ending up in the circular file.

How to Do It

Remember, your paper work needs to be persuasive, to look like sales copy. With this in mind, you need to follow four simple guidelines for composing these first glimpses of your identity.

Paragraph One: State the purpose of your letter and how it is you came to approach this person (e.g., response to an ad, job posting).

Paragraph Two: Briefly summarize your major attributes including skills, knowledge areas, areas of expertise, and so on. Choose those that will be of most interest to this particular audience.

Paragraph Three: Briefly state what you know about them. Have you ever heard of a vacuum cleaner salesman who didn't talk about your rugs? This is your first opportunity to show your audience that you are aware of and care about their needs.

Paragraph Four: Make a short statement about why you think you and the organization would make a good match. This is your chance to clinch an interview. If you can tie their needs to your skills, you're almost sure to get a response. Remember, most people don't write this kind of letter.

Sample Cover Letter (Use this when responding to a vacancy.)

January 6, 1989

Mr. Harold Hamlin
Director of Human Resources
Rainbow Computer Company
Rainbow Drive
Dallas, TX 17654

Dear Mr. Hamlin:

I am writing in response to your search for a Manager in Human Resource Development. I became aware of your search to fill this position through the *New York Times* and a job posting in my current company.

My experience in human resource management, team management, personnel policy administration, and project management qualify me for the position. In addition, my experience handling human resource allocation problems in the past and my track record for resolving tricky personnel problems provide me with the skills critical to making a significant contribution.

From my perspective, your company has always stood for high quality. Even during transition periods, when other companies questioned Rainbow's capacity to endure, there seemed to be a sense that product integrity came first.

I am sure that a key ingredient to maintaining the level of quality Rainbow is known for is in the people who work there. I suspect it is attention to the human resource that gives you your competitive edge. I, too, believe that attention to the needs of people, their problems, and the resolution of those problems makes the difference between an average company and an excellent one. My skills in human resource management, problem solving, and troubleshooting prepare me for the challenges ahead.

I would welcome the opportunity to talk with you about the possibility of working with you. Thank you for your consideration.

Sincerely,

Chris Simpson

Letters of Approach

Letters of approach differ from cover letters in that they don't refer to a specific job. You might use a letter of approach for gathering information, tracking leads, or getting exposure. In any case, the response you get depends on the way the letter is composed.

Because you're not selling yourself for a specific job with your letter of approach—unless you've got a hot informal lead, in which case you should treat your letter of approach as a cover letter—you can't be as direct as you would be in a cover letter. However, you still want to compel the person to talk with you. Therefore, write a letter that tells a little about you, a little about them (again, some homework may be necessary), how you came to approach them, and what you hope to gain from the conversation. This type of letter, when written well, can be remarkably effective in getting you in doors that would otherwise be locked.

A good letter is worth a thousand phone calls.

When I was working on my dissertation, I had the idea to interview prominent writers in my field of study. I approached my doctoral committee with this list of impressive names, and they expressed concern that I wouldn't be able to get access to these people. But having coached many people on letters of approach, I was confident I could write some that would open doors for me. The committee eventually agreed—after all, it was my neck—but told me to create a backup list in case I failed to get to my top ten. One committee member, dubious about my chances, voiced concern that I should not end up with a second-class list of experts. He suggested I try calling these people first to see what my chances were. I disagreed.

Early success in risky ventures is important to keep you going, so I began my research by approaching the two people I thought would be most responsive and least unreachable. I spent some time reading what I could about these people, talking to anyone and everyone who might know something about them, and thinking about the best way to get them to want to see me.

Once I felt confident that I knew my audience, I began writing. I told each of them why I was approaching them, what I found interesting about them (a little subdued buttering up never hurts), and what I hoped to gain from our conversation. In the end, eight of my original ten agreed to see me. (One said to try again in two months, and one said she was too busy.) During my dissertation defense, my dubious committee member asked one final question, "How did you get these people to see you?" I smiled and replied, "I asked."

**If you ask for what you want,
you might get it;
if you don't ask, you definitely won't.**

How to Do It

Paragraph One: Describe what you are approaching them for, how it is you came to approach them in particular (i.e., common acquaintance, recent publicity, knowledge of their expertise, or reputation in their field).

Paragraph Two: Describe why you think they might be interested in talking to you.

Paragraph Three: Describe what it is about them that makes you want to talk with them.

Paragraph Four: Explain in general terms what you hope to gain from the conversation.

Sample Letter of Approach (Use this when seeking information, visibility, and making contacts.)

April 20, 1988

Ms. Charlotte Howard
Human Resource Manager
International Computer
600 Hanover Street
Philadelphia, PA 09885

Dear Ms. Howard:

I am approaching you at the suggestion of our mutual acquaintance Janet Spandler. After eleven years in the paper industry, I am considering making a transition into the high-technology field. Janet thought you might be interested in hearing about my situation and might be able to help me navigate my way.

Over the years, I have worked in the area of human resources in a variety of capacities and have developed a broad range of skills. At this point, I am exploring the extent to which those skills are transferable from the paper industry to the computer industry. I'm sure there are some similarities and some differences.

Your name came up in my conversation with Janet as someone who has seen the human resource function from a variety of perspectives. I have also heard of you and your work from other sources in the course of my early exploration. From what I've heard, you strike me as the kind of person who really has a grasp of your profession.

I would like fifteen minutes of your time to ask you some very specific questions about your business, your thoughts on the kind of transition I'm thinking about, and, if I decide to pursue this direction, possible leads for work.

I will call you the week of May 1 to arrange, if you are willing, a time for us to talk. Thank you for your consideration.

Sincerely,

Chris Simpson

Letters and Gatekeepers

One of the best things a letter can do for you is to get you through the elaborate maze that busy people create around themselves to keep unwanted visitors away. You should end your letter by saying that you will call to follow up on your request. Then, when the gatekeeper, usually a secretary or assistant, asks if the person is expecting your call, you say yes. And *voilà*, you've made it through the gate and are on your way to a face-to-face meeting.

A Note on Thank-You Letters

Thank-you letters are a good thing. They show the person you've spoken with that you are courteous and that you appreciate the time they have given you. (If you can tell them specifically what you appreciated in addition to their time, all the better.) A thank-you letter also reminds the person on the other end of your existence and your needs. Use them whenever they seem appropriate. A word of warning: Don't go overboard. I recently got a letter from a woman thanking me for just agreeing to see her!

"O": OCCUPATIONAL INVESTIGATION

Information is the currency of modern life. Just as products were the fuel of the industrial society and property was the fuel of the agrarian society, information is the fuel of the service society.

There are many signs of this emerging reality. Those with the information have the power. The success of the entire computer industry is based on a company's ability to design products that can process more information faster. Information is money. Last year, Digital Equipment Corporation launched a marketing campaign called DECWORLD, a one-time event costing $20 million. Its purpose: to disseminate information about its new products. The company expects to make a profit of $1 billion as a result. In recent years, the financial world has been rocked by insider-trading scandals. The cause: the wrong people having the right information at the wrong time. In 1985, when Bruce Springsteen was at the peak of his popularity, his fame was demonstrated by an incident in Washington, D.C. Within hours after tickets for one of his concerts went on sale, the Washington phone lines were so overloaded by people trying to get them that the entire phone system was shut down. More than Springsteen's popularity was at work; the reality of the information society was highlighted by the speed with which word about his concerts spread. The prospect of seeing his show stopped the flow of information almost instantly in one of the most important information exchange networks in the world.

Because information has become such a priceless commodity, expertise in information gathering and retrieval is necessary for achieving and maintaining success in the career marketplace. Regardless of the arena you're in, having the right information at the right time can make the difference between success and failure. Your capacity to gather information, process it, and use it will determine the extent to which you can make moves that are timely, appropriate, and likely to satisfy you.

The Compelling Job Market

For years, career counselors, recruiters, and career books have talked about the "hidden job market." I've never liked the term and what it implies. There is no hidden market, and people attuned to the marketplace need not spend time trying to uncover one. They need only utilize their resources to get the offers they want.

**There is no hidden job market,
only people in hiding.**

What most people lack is not the key to unlocking the hidden market, but the attention and action required to discover the range of opportunities already available. Another reason I don't like the hidden job market concept is that it implies someone is purposely hiding the good jobs. All indications are that during the 1990s and early twenty-first century, there will be an intense labor shortage in many fields, and talented people will be able to choose the work they want. The trick will be paying attention to your options and keeping your eye on the ball. This is very simple (although not necessarily easy) and requires using all your senses.

Conquering the Compelling Market
Through the Senses

The Eyes

Many people complain that they can't seem to find information about the kinds of occupations, organizations, and fields that would lead them to good work. What they don't realize is that the information is literally at their fingertips. The person who most vividly illustrates this point, I think, is John Naisbitt, author of the best-selling *Megatrends*. Naisbitt has built a staggeringly successful business and has become one of the country's leading futurists simply by using his eyes. What he did to amass the wealth of information presented in *Megatrends*, information that seems more accurate as time goes on, was to establish a pattern of reading local newspapers from all parts of the country to identify emergent trends.

Using his eyes (and the eyes of his staff), Naisbitt was able to track events by reading about them. He was then able to formulate uncannily accurate conclusions about a vast range of world events.

If you scale down Naisbitt's approach to finding one job for one person, you will have the technology for uncovering the information about the jobs you want. In other words, read anything and everything you can about your area of interest, and you will find out all you need to know to move forward. The key here is establishing and maintaining your focus. Once you're focused on a particular area, it's remarkable how the data start to flow. Say, for example, that you just bought a blue Firebird. I'll bet that until you owned one, you never noticed how many blue Firebirds there are. Now, however, they seem to pop up everywhere you go. Once you focus on something, anything, your attention is programmed to it, and it continues to appear, almost by magic. Of course, you don't want to rely exclusively on magic. Make sure that in addition to reading newspapers, you look at other sources of information likely to give you clues to your chosen occupation—magazines, trade journals, government reports, books. A good librarian can show you where the best materials are for your interests.

The Ears

Your ability to listen to what's going on around you can provide you with immense amounts of knowledge in your chosen area. The most obvious and accessible sources for information via the ears are the electronic media: radio and television. To get the most from these most powerful icons of the information age, you need to be selective. Pee Wee Herman can teach you about life in the fast lane, and programs like "Cheers" can teach you proper after-work etiquette, but the most popular network fare will do little to advance your career. Your best bet for valuable information is to focus on public broadcasting stations, all-news stations (both radio

and cable), stations that emphasize personal and professional development programming, and occasional network
news specials on pressing issues. Choosing to focus some of
the time you spend with the tube or the radio on your occupational investigation can prove worthwhile in a number of
surprising ways.

When we think about where we hear valuable information,
the first things that come to mind in this media-absorbed age
are TV and radio. But a great deal of information can be
gained by placing yourself in the presence of people who do
the kind of work you're interested in and just listening to
them. Going to meetings, conferences, workshops, classes,
seminars, and even parties attended by people who do the
kind of work you're thinking about can provide an enormous
amount of information about that line of work. More important, surrounding yourself with these people will give you
clues to whether you could thrive in their culture. (More on
this in "Casing the Culture," in Chapter 7.)

The Mouth

Eventually, the early stages of your investigation will yield
enough information that you will want to delve deeper into
some of the questions that have come up. This means talking to people. Some of you have been eager to get to this
stage; others have been terrified of it.

People have always relied on others to help them figure
out what to do with their lives. Some would say that is what
the whole process of education is—or should be—about.
About twenty years ago, John Crystal, one of the founding
fathers of career development strategy, introduced the idea
of educating yourself about a job area before entering it. This
idea was echoed by Richard Bolles in his enduring *What
Color Is Your Parachute?* One of the strategies developed by
Bolles and others was the notion of the *informational interview*: talking to people who do what you would like to do to
find guidance in your pursuit of new work. Although the term

itself has been overused and the practice abused (it is not supposed to be a sneaky way of getting a job interview), the concept is still sound. Bolles continues to recommend it but suggests that you not call it informational interviewing when you approach prospective interviewees. Regardless of what you call it, it's important that you do it before you pursue actual positions in a particular field. Ask people in that line of work a few simple questions: what they like and dislike about their work, how they got started, how they would proceed if they were trying to break into the field today, and what opportunities they see for work in that field in the future. Their responses will tell you all you need to know to proceed, including where to apply for jobs, how to approach prospective employers, and whether that work is likely to be a good match for you. If, after three or four conversations, you feel good about what you've seen and heard, it's time to pursue the field further. If the conversations have left you with a bad taste in your mouth, it may be time to investigate another occupation.

The Nose and Hands

In talking about these senses as part of occupational investigation, I am of course speaking metaphorically. By using your eyes, ears, and mouth, you can uncover all the basic information you need before actually pursuing leads. What will set you apart from all the other people following this very logical path is developing a *nose for news* and a *Midas touch*. The nose for news comes into play when you're looking for unusual avenues of access to potential positions. Paying attention to the marketplace you're looking into can give you clues about job possibilities. Any major change in an organization usually means a change in personnel. If a company is moving into your area, chances are some of its people won't be coming along, and that means jobs. If a company has just bought another firm or even put up a new building, that probably means new jobs. If someone has just been promoted or hired for a high-level position, they probably want some hand-picked players for support. Many of the changes that occur in organizations can create conditions leading to new jobs. Developing a nose for those changes can make the difference between catching and missing a golden opportunity.

Tapping these golden opportunities often requires a Midas touch, an approach somewhere between forcing yourself on a potential employer and operating in obscurity. Once you have sniffed out those unique opportunities, your approach will make all the difference. If in your occupational research you uncover a potential job (this happens quite often) and are genuinely interested in pursuing it, you must approach the situation carefully. People in a position to hire have their typical ways of getting talent. You will have to convince them that the path that led you to them is worthy of their attention. Use your persuasive paper work skills and write a letter that can't be ignored, or tap your network (more about networks later in this chapter) for someone to get you in the door for ten minutes. For either approach to be effective, you need to have the goods, to be able to tell them what you have to offer that is unique.

The Sixth Sense

Beyond the five basic senses is the sixth sense, intuition. Much has been written in recent years about the use of intuition in business, psychology, and the arts. There is in fact a wellspring of interest in the subject, much of it articulated in writings on New Age thinking. The basic concept is simple: There is a force within each of us that helps us to understand the world. Summoning up the intuitive aspect of your psyche, which helps you make judgments about your experience beyond the facts, can be a very powerful tool in your occupational research.

The most vivid example I know of the sixth sense at work was told to me by an artist friend. While he was a professor at the University of Mississippi, he lived in a house owned by the then-unknown primitive painter Theora Hamblett. Ms.

Hamblett painted for her own pleasure until my friend, a formidable art analyst, encouraged her to show her work to some New York critics. She soon became well known in her field. Much of her work came out of what she referred to as "visions of her childhood."

One day, a man called from the University of Mississippi to arrange for a showing of her work. Ms. Hamblett agreed, and shortly thereafter the man, appropriately dressed and not particularly suspicious-looking, arrived and picked up forty paintings. As he left with the paintings, Ms. Hamblett had what she referred to as "a vision" that something was not right, that her paintings were in the wrong hands. She called the university to confirm the plans for the show and was told there were none. Her paintings were retrieved on the Gulf Coast on their way to India!

Call it vision, insight, intuition, or whatever, the ability to see beyond what appears to be to what really is, is a talent some are born with and some need to cultivate. Ms. Hamblett sensed danger as it was unfolding and was able to avert irreparable damage to both her career and her heart. This capacity to see beyond the surface is critical to success in your career. If you have it, use it; if you don't yet have it, develop it.

Most of the techniques for occupational research involve common sense, but some, such as intuition, involve uncommon sense. It is important to realize that there are many potential benefits and liabilities connected to *any* career choice. The challenge is to approach the investigation with all your senses heightened in order to assure that once you've decided what to pursue, you're as certain as it is possible to be that you've made the right choice.

"I": INFLUENTIAL INTERVIEWING

**Most people spend their time
worrying about the wrong things.**

Interviewing is both an art and a science. Because it is something people do only when they are in transition, they don't get a lot of practice. The basics of interviewing—the science part—are mostly common sense and do not need much elaboration. Here are some tips for making sure you have a grasp of the basics.

Ten Tips for a Better Job Interview: The Science of Interviewing

1. Do Your Homework

People who study the organization with which they are interviewing do well in the interview. They are able to ask intelligent questions that demonstrate their genuine interest in the job, and they can relate their skills to the specific needs of the potential employer.

2. Be Physically Prepared

This may seem obvious, but a lot of people overlook it anyway. Be sure to get a good night's sleep before an interview and eat a good breakfast. It is much harder to perform well if you're tired and hungry. Also be sure you dress appropriately; the rule of thumb is one step dressier than your usual on-the-job clothing.

3. Practice Interviewing

This is a good way to get rid of the jitters, sharpen your delivery, and relax. Choose someone you feel comfortable with, and hold a mock interview. If you're feeling particularly nervous, think about the questions that make you most nervous and practice answering them until you feel more comfortable with your responses. Remember, everyone gets nervous in interviews. The more you practice, the more confident you'll feel, and the more relaxed you'll be.

4. Respond Calmly to Stressful Questions

Interviewers sometimes ask impossible questions just to see how you handle stress. The *way* you react to such questions is as important as the answers you give. Remember, you don't have to have all the answers; you just need to be able to handle all the questions.

5. Maintain a Balance of Talking and Listening

Make sure you talk enough to present a full picture of yourself, but don't talk so much that the interviewer feels you're monopolizing the conversation. There's no rule of thumb here; fifty-fifty doesn't always work. Your best bet is to be attentive and let your interviewer take the lead.

6. Think Before You Speak

Most people dread the moments of silence between question and answer. Don't be afraid to sit and think for a while. Good questions require thoughtful answers, and bad questions require creative responses.

7. Never (almost never) Turn Down the Opportunity for an Interview

Even if you don't want the position, take the interview. It will be good practice and you might find out about another position that would be a better match. Also, if you make a good impression, you may be called back to interview for something more attractive.

The only time to decline an interview is when there is direct cost involved for the potential employer (e.g., airfare). If you aren't really interested in the position and they sense that, they will not offer you anything else and will rightfully resent your wasting their money.

8. Expect the Unexpected

Don't expect to talk to just one person; group interviews are common, as are consecutive one-to-one interviews. The best way to treat a series of one-to-one interviews is to assume that none of your interviewers speak to one another and therefore that each needs to see the whole picture. The best way to treat a group interview is as if it is a series of one-to-one interviews. Try to make contact with each person in the group. Also, assume that the person asking you a particular question is the one most interested in your response.

9. Be Enthusiastic

Many interviewers get tired of the process and lose some of their enthusiasm. This can be contagious. Don't get caught up in their lack of enthusiasm. If you sense you're sitting across from a worn-out interviewer, be especially energetic. This, too, can become contagious.

10. Take All the Time You Need (within reason)

If you get an offer and you're not sure you want the job, don't feel pressured to give an answer on the spot. Take twenty-four hours to think it over. If they want you, they'll wait. If they won't wait, it's probably a good indication that you don't want to work for them.

These ten points will provide you with basic information on the science of interviewing. But by themselves, they will not make you stand out in the crowd, which is what you really want. The way to stand out and get the job offers you want is to master the *art* of interviewing.

The Art of Interviewing

Effective interviewing involves leaving the interviewer with two things: a vivid picture of your abilities and a feeling of being connected with you as a person. These two aspects are worth some elaboration because:

Talented people get praise;
persuasive people get jobs.

No matter how good you are at what you do, if you can't persuade someone of your value in the short time allotted to you, you will be out of luck. Chances are the job will go to someone who couldn't do half the job you could but is better at closing the deal.

Let's consider the vivid picture of your abilities first. Research on influence and persuasion suggests that people remember and are impressed by images more than words. That's why, when you go to a resort to look at buying into a time-sharing offer, they show you pictures of exotic members from all over the world. It's also why the vacuum cleaner salesperson not only talks about your rugs but dumps dirt on them and cleans it up. This simple concept is the basis for most marketing, including the marketing of oneself.

In an interview, a picture
***is* worth a thousand words.**

Since you can't bring pictures of yourself at work to an interview, you need to provide images through verbal means— that is, with stories.

A Piece of Chicken, Some Fries, and Good Conversation

In one of my previous careers, I was a human resource trainer. One of the questions I could anticipate when applying for a job was, "How well do you handle people who are resistant to being trained?" The first few times I was asked this question, I gave a typical response, such as, "I am good at breaking down resistance and winning people over." Although this identified a couple of my skills, it lacked pizzazz and, I suspected, left my interviewer with no lasting impression of my real capacity to handle difficult trainees.

After losing out on several jobs that I knew I could have gotten, I began to rethink my approach to such questions. I realized that I was not *showing* them I was good at breaking down barriers; I was merely telling them. Research on listening suggests:

The average person spends 50 to 80 percent of his/her day listening, hears only half of that, understands one quarter, and remembers even less.

The challenge is to provide the interviewer with a vivid picture of your abilities in a certain area, something that will get his or her attention and leave a lasting impression. The following story is one I began telling to illustrate my abilities at working with difficult trainees.

One of my jobs working for the Connecticut Department of Human Resources was to provide communication-skills training to what were then called CAP (Community Action Program) agencies. One agency in New Haven was particularly resistant to receiving any training. After trying for several weeks, I was finally able to set up a three-hour session. I arrived at 1:30 for our 2:00-5:00 workshop. By 2:20, no one had yet arrived, and I began to get nervous. As I was packing to leave at 2:45, people began arriving. Because setting up the meeting had been quite a chore, I decided to stay and give it a shot. Most of the group arrived carrying shopping bags of Kentucky Fried Chicken. As I was about to begin, one woman said, "You don't mind if we eat while you talk, do you?" I thought for a moment and said, "Not as long as I can have a piece of chicken, some fries, and some good conversation." They all laughed, gave me some food, and we spent the rest of the session talking about their frustration over the irrelevance of prior training to their work. In the end, they asked me to come back the following week to do the training originally planned. My association with that group was one of the most productive training relationships I had at that job.

This story does several things. It gives the interviewer a vivid picture of some of my prior work, demonstrates my ability to handle difficult situations, attests to my commitment to my work, and finally, makes him/her laugh. I have used it in countless situations, and it has always gotten results. One time—as I learned afterward—it was the deciding factor in a final hiring decision.

Everyone has stories about getting out of difficult situations that illustrate their abilities more than simple words can do. Dig your stories out, and tell them every chance you get.

Style: More Than Just Clothes and Manners

The Department of Labor, Bureau of Labor Statistics conducted a study in which they asked managers, "When you have two people who are equally qualified for a position, how do you determine which one you will choose?"

Eighty percent of the respondents said something to this effect: "There was just something about them. I had a feeling for them. They just seemed like the right fit." All these responses amount to the same thing: The interviewer picks the person with whom he or she feels the strongest connection. If this is so, you have to pay attention to style and respond to your interviewer in a way that gets through his or her *style screen*.

A style screen is a kind of filter. Think, for example, of several people who observe a car accident. Each reports a different chain of events when describing the same incident— an example of how perception alters one's view of reality. One common explanation for the discrepancies in their stories is the idea that everyone has a perceptual screen that filters information. Similarly, it seems that everyone has a style screen, a point of view through which they filter their experiences of other people. (See "Preferred Work Styles" in Chapter 2 for more on this.)

Because an interview is an artificial setting that by its very nature limits clear communication, it is essential that you take style screens and their impact on making a connection that counts into consideration. Let's take the example of the human resource trainer. Imagine that the interviewer asks the following question: "I noticed in your last job you were a project manager. Would you outline the steps you took when starting a new project?"

The first thing to do when attempting to penetrate someone's style screen is to analyze their question and determine what style it reflects. In this case, the interviewer is evidently taking a methodical approach, asking you to "outline the steps."

Now if your preferred style is interactive, or if you're just in an interactive mood that day, you may say, "Well, I simply got all the people involved together, we figured out what we needed to do and who needed to do what, and we did it."

Congratulations! You've just fallen flat on your face. The chances of getting serious consideration from your response to that question are nil. You should have given your answer within the interviewer's context of the question rather than go with you own inclination at the moment. Because the interviewer's style context for that question was methodical, the answer should have been methodical.

Now, some of you are probably saying, "But that's not being honest. I should answer the way I want to." That's your prerogative, and you can talk to each other about it on the unemployment line. If you want to make that tenuous but critical connection with your interviewer, you need to get past his or her style screen. You are not being dishonest; you are merely describing yourself in terms that are likely to be understood and remembered.

Let's look at the same situation in reverse. The interviewer says, "I noticed in your last position that you were a project manager. That must have meant juggling a lot of personalities. How did you manage to do that?"

A quick analysis of this question will tell you that the interviewer is in an interactive mode. He wants to know how you manage relationships or "juggle personalities." Imagine that you say, "First, I conducted a needs assessment to determine individual requirements. Second, I compiled the data from the needs assessment. Third, I analyzed the data...." Even though you may have approached the situation in a highly effective manner, chances are your response is going to leave your interviewer cold—and you out in the cold.

Interviewing is a very imperfect forum for assessing a person's potential. Even the most experienced interviewers have to make decisions based on very limited information. Therefore, you need to make sure that as much information as possible gets conveyed in the most palatable way. Paying attention to style is one way to enhance your chances of being heard and influencing your interviewer in your direction. Your ability to influence your interviewer is critical to the results. Remember:

**In the interview game, you need to feel
evenly matched; but remember,
you're playing on their home court.**

Learn to listen for style, and you will be much more likely to give responses that motivate the interviewer to want to know more about you. Here is a reference key for interpreting the style frame of various types of interview questions.

Interview Style Reference Key

Interactive: Questions that elicit responses about relationships, feelings, and attitudes are characteristic of an interactive style. The best way to respond to these questions is to address the "people management" side of the particular task or situation being discussed.

Practical: Questions that elicit responses about results, final outcomes, and achievements are characteristic of a practical style. The best way to respond is to present specific information about a given activity's outcome or result.

Methodical: Questions that elicit responses about procedures, strategies, and methods are characteristic of a methodical style, as are questions that ask for an "outline" or "review" of steps. The best way to respond to such questions is with a step-by-step description of your actions.

Creative: Questions that elicit responses about ideas, possibilities, and values are characteristic of a creative style. The best way to respond to this type of question is to enter into a discussion of beliefs or to explore the possibilities of a particular idea. (Which tack you take here depends on the nature of the question; the important thing is to be willing to delve into the unknown.)

Being Your Most Appropriate Self

Some people are intimidated by the interview process and expend most of their energy trying to second-guess the interviewer in order to "give them what they want." Other people, determined not to be intimidated, present their unexpurgated selves regardless of their impact on the interviewer. The most effective approach to interviewing is somewhere between these two extremes. You need to present a realistic view of who you are, but you also need to pay attention to what the interviewer is looking for and the context in which he/she is looking for it. Sharpening your capacity to balance these two aspects of an interview will lead to the emergence of many more options and the delivery of many more offers.

An interview is no different from any other social situation. There is much to be said for presenting an authentic view of yourself regardless of the context, but if you want to be seen as attractive, the *way* you present yourself is worth consideration. You need to adapt to the circumstances of the situation, and in fact, you do this every day. If you're like most people, your authentic self behaves differently when you are alone, with your parents, your co-workers, your children, your friends, your spouse, your ex-spouse. In all these situations, you can be yourself, but the circumstances influence how you behave. Identifying, understanding, and adapting to the circumstances of a particular interview can make the difference between your authentic self being accepted and rejected. Remember:

**Who you are matters,
but what they see also matters.**

"N": NETWORKING

If information is the currency of the service society, networking is the technology. Learning to use this technology to its fullest extent can make the difference between prosperity and destitution.

A friend of mine vividly experienced the power of networking recently. A vice president of a medium-sized company, he was experiencing a great deal of frustration with his new president. It seemed that every time he approached his new boss, he was hastily shuffled off to talk to an assistant. Worried that he was being groomed for the exit ramp, my friend tapped his formidable network, including an elaborate computer-linked web of professionals all across the country. Using his computer terminal, he posed several questions about his situation and requested a response from anyone who was interested. Within twenty-four hours, he received seven responses. Six outlined strategies for dealing with a situation such as his. The payoff came with the seventh response; it was from a man who happened to be an old friend of the vice president's new boss. The message was that the new president was having difficulties with his aging parents. The advice was to lay low and see if things improved. Eventually, it became clear that the vice president was not in trouble and that the problems were the president's personal ones and had nothing to do with work. Had my friend not tapped his network for help, he could have ended up creating trouble where there was none.

Networking can be a powerful thing. You don't need access to a sophisticated computer; all you need to do is use your potential to create linkages for gathering information. When people tell me they have no network, I ask them if they have an insurance agent, a hairdresser, a doctor, a relative, or a friend. If they have any one of these, they have access to a network. Most people have networks that are much richer than this, and if they don't, they can create them very easily.

One of the things I do in my seminars is to create an informal networking gathering once people have decided on directions they want to pursue. The rules are simple: Each person tapes a piece of paper with their top three interests listed on it to their lapel and walks around the room. The goal is to provide others with a contact for one or more of their interests. The activity is stopped when each person has gotten at least three contacts. It never takes more than twenty minutes. Although most people are not in situations where they can wear their desires on their sleeves, this exercise demonstrates how accessible contacts, information, and opportunities are if only they are pursued.

Most people employ this concept in other parts of their lives without thinking about it. How many people would pick a plumber, electrician, lawyer, physician, or baby-sitter out of the phone book, without referrals from someone who knows the person's work? Yet most people rely on the newspaper for their job leads. The fact is:

**Right now you have access to someone
who has a good job for you.**

The problem is that they don't know someone with your talents and interests is looking for work. They may not even know you, but there's a good chance that there's someone the two of you know in common who could bridge the gap between what you're looking for in a job and what they're looking for in an employee. People keep their career plans under a shroud because they are concerned their current bosses will find out, and by doing so, they miss opportunities left and right.

Just as the gathering of information is the key to occupational research, the disseminating of information about your skills, accomplishments, potential, and interests is the key to networking. Although networking can help you gain valuable information (as in the case of the worried vice president), the primary function of networking at this stage of the POINT Process is to get information about you into the hands of the people who have the power to hire you.

There are many formal and informal avenues for networking.

Formal Angles

Organizations   Newsletters

Clubs   Lectures

Conferences   Newspapers

Coalitions   Seminars

By spending time with people who work in the field you're interested in, you can gain exposure, make contacts, and get those critical leads that may eventually result in new work. The most important aspect of this type of networking is broadcasting your needs in this new arena. Simply put, when you go to these organizations, clubs, and conferences, let people know why you are there and what you are looking for. You may find you are what they are looking for. Also, you can gain insight into what the people you're interested in working with want in an employee by reading the materials they use to broadcast their success. Another way to gain exposure is to appear in some of this literature. Imagine the headway you could make if you wrote an article for a newsletter in your area of interest. It's not as difficult as you might think. Most professional and trade publications need material to fill their issues. If you have decent writing skills and a real interest in the field, you have a good chance of getting an article placed. Another way to get attention through the written word is to advertise yourself in appropriate places. People in some fields are particularly receptive to this avenue and read ads as a form of scouting. To discern whether people in the field you're approaching operate that way, check their journals' and newsletters' classified sections. The larger and more sophisticated the self-promotion section is, the more likely that it is taken seriously.

Informal Angles

The Grapevine	Travel
Friends	Parties
Relatives	Business Associates
Clergy	Service Providers

Probably the richest source for your networking activities is informal contacts, people you know or encounter who, by the nature of what they do, know a lot of other people. Letting these contacts know what you're looking for and asking their help in making connections is often all you need to get to the right people. Tap this rich source of possibilities and you will never be lacking for your next lead.

Robert T.: From Bad Knees to Good News

Robert T. was an auto body repairman—from all local accounts, one of the best in the business. About a year ago, he began experiencing knee problems. His doctor told him that his knees were "going bad" and that he would eventually have to give up his occupation. Rob didn't know what to do. The only experience he had aside from breathing new life into old wrecks was as a Boy Scout leader.

After several weeks of exploring possibilities, Rob decided to investigate work as a vocational education teacher. He loved kids, and he certainly knew his trade. So he tapped his network and got in touch with an acquaintance (another Scout leader) who was on one of the local school boards. That person put him in touch with a local vocational technical teacher, who put him in touch with a principal.

This principal told him that he needed some additional schooling to get certified and that the market was tight. Rob then talked to people at other schools in the area and always got the same response: They wouldn't touch him without certification. Before giving up, Rob spoke to the vocational education department in every high school within a fifty-mile radius. At this point, his auto body business was booming, and his knees were feeling okay, so he decided to put his career plans on hold.

About two weeks later, Rob got a call from one of the principals he had spoken with. It seemed one of their teachers had to resign abruptly, and they were strapped for a replacement. They agreed to take Rob on provisionally, with the understanding that he would complete the certification requirements as soon as possible. This opportunity, the result of his massive networking campaign, was enough motivation for him to make a shift. He now teaches full time and supplements his teaching salary with a part-time auto body parts business.

Sorry, You're Not Qualified for the Position, But...

You may think that Rob's situation was a fluke, but it wasn't. One of the key benefits of networking is increased exposure. When I first got out of college, I had a hard time finding a job because English teachers were a dime a dozen then. After a couple of months of searching, I decided to respond to an ad for a special education position. Even though I didn't have the stated qualifications, I figured the exposure wouldn't hurt. A former classmate who was teaching in that system helped me get in the door. After lengthy interviews with several people, the assistant superintendent offered me the position. "Of course," he said, "you have the proper certification."

I said, "No, I don't."

"Then why did you apply for the position?"

I replied, "I thought you might make an exception if you really wanted me."

He explained that the restriction was a legal one and sent me on my way.

Six months later, I got a call from the same assistant superintendent asking if I was interested in an English opening they had. Since I was working in a job outside my field at the time, I jumped at the offer. My work there was very satisfying until I decided that teaching school wasn't for me.

The significant thing about Rob's story and mine is that neither of us would have gotten our jobs if we had not extended our web of contacts to every place that might possibly want us. Had we not networked effectively in spite of our lack of qualifications, we never would have gotten the offers because the employers in need would never have known we existed.

If you really work on expanding, cultivating, and maintaining your network of contacts, opportunities will come your way when you least expect them. Some people would frown upon trying to get work for which they didn't have the proper credentials. They, too, can talk about their feelings on the unemployment line. These two stories show that even in schools, one of the most credential-conscious arenas there is, there are ways around the formal barriers. Good people are hard to find. If you can demonstrate that you're a worthwhile employee, people will find a way to hire you. From my point of view:

Networking is far better than not working.

"T": TRACKING LEADS

This is where you take all that you've learned from your occupational investigation and your networking and fine-tune your ability to follow and make the most of leads. It is the part of the process where you have to use your intuitive abilities and pay attention to all your hunches. The unlikely can become the norm if you really put your feelers out. Knowing when to follow a lead and when to pass one by is a skill in itself and requires both your ability to analyze situations and your capacity to tap your intuition.

Setting Yourself Apart

Howard G.: From the Slow Road to the Fast Track

Howard G. was a general manager of an industrial supply company. Because shrinking demand for his product was a constant threat to his livelihood, he decided to pursue work in the computer industry. While attending classes one night (he was finishing his M.B.A.), he saw a notice that the new manager of a local computer assembly plant was speaking on the innovative management system in operation at the plant. He made a snap decision to cut his class for three reasons: First, his instincts led him to believe that there might be some unknown opportunities on the horizon. Second, he supposed that since this manager was new to the plant, he might be looking to bring in some people of his own. Third, the plant sounded like a place that would value creative approaches to managing people, an area that Howard was studying.

The seminar turned out to be very informative. Howard learned a lot about the new organization and the new manager's approach. At the end of the session, he was about to approach the speaker, résumé in hand, when he noticed about ten other people doing the same thing. Instead of approaching the speaker, Howard decided to go home and write a letter. In the letter, he told the manager what he learned from the speech and how he was planning to apply some of the principles to his current work. He also asked if it would be possible to get a tour of the plant to learn more about what seemed to be "winning strategies." He followed up the letter with a phone call informing the secretary that the manager had invited him to tour the facility (an offer made to the group at the seminar). When told that group tours were being arranged in conjunction with interviews for new positions, Howard declined to sign up. Because he didn't have any computer experience, he felt he wasn't ready for a competitive interview.

A few days later, Howard called the manager again. This time he approached by saying he was a student who had seen the presentation the previous week and had decided to do a paper for his management class on this innovative plant (not untrue). He was granted an interview for the paper and, in the end, was offered the position he wanted.

The lesson to be learned from Howard's careful maneuvering is, not that the way to success is through deceit, but that the way to get what you want is to set yourself apart from the crowd and highlight your uniqueness.

Carl H.: Turning a Long Shot into a Sure Bet

One of the most remarkable lead-tracking stories I know is about a man who started his search knowing nothing of the possibilities, but who played out each step and is now in a position to create a major business and introduce a new crop to a region in need of farming alternatives. The man, whom I'll call Carl, lives in Europe and works in his family's produce business. Learning that the bulk of this crop consumed in the United States is imported, he decided to pursue the possibility of growing it in the States. The first thing he did was to broadcast his intent by writing a letter to the port authority of every state in the country. He received one positive inquiry from a woman involved in economic development for her region. He set up a meeting with her to talk about whether the crop could grow in the region and, if so, whether it would sell there. The woman sensed the possibilities for the region's economic development and agreed to help in any way she could. From this beginning, the principals involved have received federal funding for crop development and market research, and the project is well on its way to becoming a reality. If it succeeds, it will benefit all the parties involved.

Tracking Leads Through Effective Patterning

What these two stories have in common is the essence of successful tracking patterns. Starting with only a hint of possibility, both Howard and Carl were able to create their own success.

Analyzing their patterns will help clarify the strategy for tracking leads. First, each **identified a possibility**: getting a job in a particular plant, growing a new crop in a different country. Next, they **gathered information**: what the organization is like, who would be interested in crop development. Next, they **broadcast their intentions**: to learn more about the organization, gain access to management, and ultimately get a job; to develop a new crop and business for a new region. Each **invited a response** through a phone call or meeting. Then each **assessed the response**: Carl, gaining the response he wanted, **continued tracking**; Howard, unhappy with the prospect of getting lost in the shuffle, had to **regroup and reframe** his approach to get the individual attention he wanted from the key manager. Next, each **pursued additional leads:** Howard got his job; Carl is waiting for the results of his research before deciding whether to set up shop or jump to another track.

On the next page is a model outlining the key steps of an effective lead-tracking pattern.

The key to effective tracking is the ability to adapt your pattern to the requirements of the situation. Many people give up as soon as a lead doesn't pan out the way they envisioned it. Unlike Howard, who reframed his approach when he didn't like where it was leading him, unsuccessful trackers accept the first response they get as the only one possible. The way to successfully track leads to jobs is to move systematically through the series of steps outlined in the lead-tracking pattern. This does not mean that everything will go your way. But you'll be making the most of your leads and assessing what you need to do next. Use this system to track and follow up on leads and opportunities that you never dreamed possible will come your way.

Don't Start from Scratch

If this process of tracking leads sounds exciting to you, begin using it now. If it sounds intimidating, you may want to avoid starting from scratch by finding a model, someone whose pattern you could emulate. This model may be a person or set of people who had needs similar to your own. Find out how they went about creating their niche, and you'll have enough information to develop your own tracking pattern.

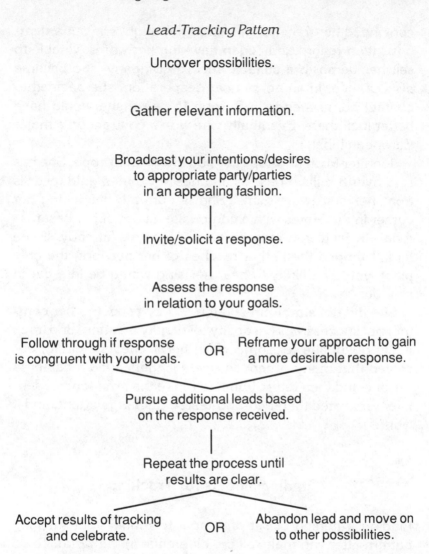

Lead-Tracking Pattern

Uncover possibilities.

Gather relevant information.

Broadcast your intentions/desires
to appropriate party/parties
in an appealing fashion.

Invite/solicit a response.

Assess the response
in relation to your goals.

Follow through if response   OR   Reframe your approach to gain
is congruent with your goals.   a more desirable response.

Pursue additional leads based
on the response received.

Repeat the process until
results are clear.

Accept results of tracking   OR   Abandon lead and move on
and celebrate.   to other possibilities.

Jennifer Rush: But Can She Sing?

A good example of someone who adapted another's tracking pattern to accomplish her own goals is Jennifer Rush.
Born in a musical family, educated at Julliard, Jennifer has a
combination seldom found in a pop singer: a great voice and
the formal training to know how to use it. When she was

convinced her material was strong enough, she cut a demonstration record and began hawking her wares. Unable to sell her demo to a suitable record company, she became discouraged. In an act of near desperation, she decided to contact some friends in Europe to see if she would have better luck there. Eventually, she won a contract on a major European label.

Jennifer Rush now tops the pop charts in Europe. She has sold over 8 million records and has seventeen gold records from her first two albums. She is currently launching her career in the States with a composite album of her best material. In fact, you may be listening to her already. If she hadn't tapped the farther reaches of her network, the only place you'd be likely to hear her sing would be in a bar in New Jersey.

She did not start from scratch. A key aspect to her commercial success was her ability to identify a pattern and track it. No doubt she (or someone in her immediate circle) observed that many American *opera* singers build a career in Europe and then return home to make their mark here. Jennifer replicated that tried-and-tested tracking pattern, and it worked.

Finding Models for Tracking

Finding a person or set of people to model your tracking pattern after can make all the difference in the world. To do so, you must look for someone who is successful at what you want to do and identify their pattern so that you can replicate or approximate it. When learning a new skill, most people do much better if they can watch someone else first and then imitate them. The same is true here. If you can find someone who has done what you're trying to do, the more you know about what they did and how they did it, the more likely you will be to succeed in your attempt.

The Tracking Model Profile lists some things to consider when trying to identify a pattern that might serve as a model for your search. Keep in mind that in all likelihood, your pattern won't be an exact replica of any one individual's; it will probably be a composite of several. The purpose of using a model is to have information that will help you to get the answers to the right questions and make decisions based in part on what others have done.

Tracking Model Profile

1. What steps did this person take to get where he/she is? _____

   _____

   _____

2. How does this person manage his/her time?

   _____

   _____

   _____

3. How does this person manage his/her money?

   _____

   _____

   _____

4. What sort of balance does this person maintain in his/her life (i.e., work, play, family, learning, fitness)?

   _____

   _____

   _____

5. What is this person's definition of success?

_____

_____

_____

6. How does this person manage relationships with people at work?

_____

_____

_____

7. What sort of support network does this person have?

_____

_____

_____

8. In what ways (if any) does this person make his/her activities known to others?

_____

_____

_____

Obviously, the answers to some of these questions will not come easily. You will get some by asking direct questions; others will come from observing the person over a period of time. Whatever it takes, it will be worth it. Completing a Tracking Model Profile of one or more people who have major aspects to their careers that you would like to replicate in your own life will give you an enormous amount of information that would take years to find out on your own. Also, the better you understand the people who do what you would like to do, the more likely your lead tracking will enable you to create and realize your own personal career track.

PART 3

TAKING HOLD

SEVEN

Signing Up

A Good Match Is Hard to Find

IN HIS autobiography, Lee Iacocca suggests that one of the most difficult managerial tasks is hiring. He says, "You never know what you're getting until you've got it." This insight is true for those on both sides of the fence.

**You never know what you're into,
until you're into it.**

Joann S.: The Case of the Mismatched Manager

Joann S. was an engineer with a large computer company, an expert in assembly technology, and bored with her work. She had successfully managed her group for four years and was looking for a new challenge. One day, she saw a notice on the bulletin board that a nearby plant was switching to a "high performance" management approach and was looking for interested internal managers.

Joann promptly signed up and made the transfer. The next six months were, as she put it, nightmarish. The "high performance" approach was a euphemism for a nonhierarchical team approach. Joann found that she was no longer a supervisor, but a team member with no special stature. Although she was a good manager in a traditional setting, her soft-spoken style left her at a disadvantage in a free-for-all environment. Joann soon became the gofer of the team, her substantial expertise all but ignored. She has since left the company and is looking for a job that better matches her style.

Joann could have avoided this damaging experience by doing some careful research before signing up.

Examining the New Turf

The investigating you do when preparing to accept an offer is similar to the type of work you would do in the occupational investigation phase of the POINT Process. However, this investigation is so important to your achieving your desired results and so different from the earlier investigating that it warrants separate attention.

Accepting an offer without examining the turf, is like buying swamp land in Florida.

Everyone knows stories of people buying bargain property sight unseen only to find out the parcel of land is not only inaccessible but unable to support a foundation. Similarly, if you're not careful in your job hunting, you may find yourself with assignments you can't accomplish and a system unable or unwilling to support your efforts. There are several angles to consider when thinking of taking a job: compatibility with the culture of the organization or, as in Joann's case, with a particular division of the organization, the health and stability of the organization, and the question of expectations (i.e., whether the job requirements are realistic and reasonable from your perspective). Let's look at each of these categories and consider various strategies for avoiding poor matches.

Casing the Culture

Most people don't realize that they can learn a lot about the culture of an organization by looking at its physical environment. If you're sitting in someone's office, you have already been exposed to many aspects of the organization. The design of the building, the ease of access to the building, the extent to which parking spaces are assigned will tell you something about the culture. Are people hurried or relaxed? Are they friendly to each other, or do they walk past one another as if they were invisible? If they do talk to one another, what do they talk about—work, play, family, world events?

Once you've arrived at your destination, you can really get a taste of the culture. Consider the office you're sitting in as a microcosm of the organization. What sort of image is the person in the office trying to convey? Is it a no-nonsense, all-business atmosphere; or is it a homey, relaxed atmosphere? Are there objects in the room hinting at life beyond the office—family pictures, sports trophies, service awards, plants—or are all the artifacts connected with work and the organization? Does your conversation with this person cover the organization, you, and the larger context in which all organizations exist, or is the focus strictly on the organization and its work?

Finally, on your way out, notice if the office you've been in is typical of the organization, or if each office is unique. Each of these clues will tell you specific things about the organization's culture and what it would be like to work in it. For example, lots with many assigned parking spaces often indicate a very hierarchical system. Most cultural artifacts by themselves will not tell you anything definitive about an organization, but a combination of three or four observations can often lead to a pretty good assessment. The important thing is to pay attention and develop your ability to paint a realistic picture of that organization. Take care, though. Culture is "in," and sometimes an organization may try to present an image that differs quite a bit from reality. I recently saw a cartoon in which a chief executive officer attending a seminar on culture turned and said to his vice president, "Culture—I like that idea—get me one by Monday!"

Obviously, true culture is more complex than that, evolving over time. If you get an impression of culture from a brief visit with an organization but feel you want more exposure before signing up, there are several things you can do. If the organization is large enough to have a cafeteria, you have the ideal place to uncover the real culture. If it doesn't have one, find out where most of the employees eat. People let their hair down when they eat—and thus provide a real view of the organization.

I remember interviewing at a large, high-tech company. After a series of meetings in the morning, I was left to my own devices for lunch—their first mistake if they really wanted me. At lunch, I met a man I'll call Ed. During our conversation about what a great company this was to work for—he was genuinely enthusiastic—he showed me a letter he had received from his seven-year-old daughter. It seemed that she was so frustrated by her father's constant absence from home that she had taken to communicating with him through the mail. Ed found his daughter's behavior cute; I found it frightening. After further discussion, I discovered that the hours he was keeping were the norm for the organization, not the exception. I learned more about what working for that organization would be like during my lunch with Ed than I did during a whole morning of formal interviews. If you find yourself in the dining hall and are not fortunate enough to meet someone like Ed, take an unobtrusive seat at the largest, fullest table you can find. Listen to what people talk about and the way they talk about it. Chances are, if people are talking about outside things, you've found an organization that doesn't devour its employees. People obsessed with their work don't take breaks. Although you can generally get a good view of an organization in this way, I caution you that it's not always so. You may have hit them at the end of a quarter or during a major project. Some organizations operate at a crisis pace all the time; joining one is fine as long as you know what you're getting into and do so willingly.

The point is, you can get a tremendous amount of raw data in the cafeteria. Once again, you need to use your analytical skills and intuition to figure out what it means and to weigh its importance.

Another cultural clue you can learn a lot from is the language organizational members use in casual conversation. During the same lunch hour I met Ed, I overheard a conversation about a marketing manager who "got hammered last night at a meeting and in the end was nailed to the wall." I don't know about you, but their meetings sound a little too violent for me. At the other extreme, a woman I know works in a manufacturing plant that is trying to function in a participatory fashion. They spend a lot of time in meetings discussing how people feel about various projects and the workings of the team. When I saw this woman last, I asked her how things were going at the plant. She said, "Right now, there's a lot of pain." Now, a typical answer about a typical plant would concern the numbers above quota the plant was producing, not the emotional climate.

Some of you would welcome the dog-eat-dog environment of the first plant and would be driven nuts by the sensitivity of the second one. For others, the opposite would be true. You may be surprised to learn that these two plants are in the same industry, manufacturing the same product—and producing about the same results.

Another way to understand the culture of an organization is to talk with anyone and everyone you encounter. One of the most informative conversations I had the day I interviewed with the high-tech company was with a temporary secretary. While waiting for one of my interviews, I asked this woman how she liked working there. She told me that the people were very nice but that there were no written guidelines for anything and that it was driving her crazy. Furthermore, when she pointed this lack out to people, it didn't seem to bother them. What this woman had done for me was to raise a red flag. I had heard about young high-tech companies that thrive on ambiguity. Their tendency to rely on verbal communication and informality attracted me; their tendency to consume the lives of their employees did not.

I also received important information by asking a personal question of one of my interviewers—a strategy I would recommend only if you've established a significant rapport with them. In this case, the common link was that we had attended the same graduate school and had studied with some of the same professors. The question I asked was, "What was it like for you when you started working here?"

My interviewer, now comfortably established in his role,

told me that after about three months on the job, he still hadn't figured out exactly what his responsibilities were. When he approached his supervisor with this concern, his supervisor responded with, "Yes, we've noticed that. And if you don't have it figured out in the next three months, you're out of here!"

This story shows that one cultural norm of this organization is to hire people and then have them figure out a way of making a contribution. Some of you would find this very exciting; others would find it horrifying. In either case, you would find it surprising if you had not done your homework.

I want to point out that I've been talking mostly about experiences I had during one day of "culture casing." I do this to highlight how accessible information about culture can be if you are open to it. Although I was lucky in some of those meetings, you can get the same kind of information if you know what to look for, and you can get it on any given day in any given organization. Here are some clues for uncovering culture.

Six Sources of Cultural Information

The Physical Environment

The physical environment encompasses all aspects of the setting of the organization, including the location, the design of the building, the layout of the building, the size and types of offices, the furniture, the art work, and all the other visible artifacts.

The Human Interaction Patterns

The human interaction patterns include the patterns of communication: who talks to whom, under what circumstances, the methods of communication (meetings, informal conversations, formal correspondence), and the range of communication (transmission of information, expression of feeling, discussion of world events and external factors influencing the organization).

Attitudes About Work and the Outside World

This information includes peoples' expressed and implied beliefs, attitudes, and values about the nature of their work, its importance, and its relationship to the rest of the world. Focus on this cultural clue will tell you the extent to which employees' view of the organization's work is integrated into the larger context in which the organization exists.

The Language Used to Describe Events

Language can provide information about the pace, integrity, standards, and priorities of the organization. The words people use to describe success, failure, and uncertainty will tell you how each of these aspects of organizational life is viewed. The words they use when discussing risk, change, conflict, and competition will show you how much these phenomena are embraced or feared.

The Physical and Mental Health of the Employees

The extent to which the people working in the organization appear and sound healthy, both physically and mentally, will give you a clue of what it might be like to work there. The level and nature of activity of the people you meet and observe can indicate the level of stress present in the organization and whether that level seems to serve as a constructive or a destructive force in the lives of the employees.

The Nature and Extent of Organization Rituals

An examination of the organization's rituals is one of the richest sources of cultural information. The extent to which the organization partakes in such rituals as parties, birthday celebrations, award celebrations, incentive programs, sports activities, training sessions, staff meetings, and staff retreats will tell you how much emphasis the leaders place on the maintenance and development of their employees.

Paying attention to these six sources of cultural information can give you a tremendous amount of information to consider before signing up with an organization. Choosing a culture that is a good fit can make all the difference in the world.

There are two things you can be certain of about culture: It exists everywhere, and it can make you or break you.

Not paying attention to culture when changing jobs is like moving to another country without knowing anything about its language, currency, or political system. Learn how to interpret culture and use the information you get to make better decisions about your prospects. Although it's true that ultimately you don't know what you're into until you're into it, there are ways to minimize your losses. It makes sense for you to do so.

Examining the Health and Stability of the Organization

The greatest culture in the world can't save you if the organization or division you've just joined is going down the tubes. Make sure the team you're about to join is in, or at least approaching, its prime. Observing the culture can sometimes tell you that, and there are other signals as well. Spend some time reading annual reports and other documentation reflecting the organization's condition. Talking with its competitors can also help; they have a major interest in the health and welfare of your prospective organization.

In addition, you want to find out about the health of the position you're about to accept. I know a man who left a good position with an oil company to accept an even better position with another oil company. When he arrived for work, he was told apologetically that "someone" was supposed to have let him know that the position had been eliminated in a reorganization. He was now out of work. I know of another man who joined a company only to find he reported to a vice president who was on his way out. The vice president saw the new hire as his last chance to prevent the inevitable. Fortunately, through some fancy footwork, my friend was able to establish his worth and avoid going down with his boss, but it doesn't always work that way. Had he done his homework, he could have avoided this near disaster. With a little informal investigation, he would have learned that this particular vice president now had only 20 people reporting to him, down from 200, and that he and the president of the company didn't get along.

Another way to flag problems is to look into the position's history. How many people prior to you have held the position, for how long, and where did they go? A position or a division with a high turnover rate should alert you to potential problems. Find out why people left and where they went—up, across, or out of the organization—and you'll have a good sense of whether you need to worry.

A sick or ailing organization is like a person in similar shape. If you watch carefully, you'll see symptoms of the disease. All organizations have problems, but it's worth your while to identify these problems and decide if you're willing to tackle them or would rather walk away.

The Zero Advancement Principle (ZAP): How to Avoid Getting ZAPped

There are many good reasons to accept a job, and many reasons to decline an offer. Many people receive offers whose only appeal is that they seem better than the job they have now or, worse, better than having no job. People are sometimes so driven by a desire to escape present dissatisfaction that they take a mediocre job and eventually end up regretting the decision.

**It is wiser to move toward a good job
than away from a bad one.**

If your only interest is moving away from what you don't want, you will see only what is different from your old job in your new prospects, not necessarily what is better. If, on the other hand, you approach the new position as an opportunity, you will have a greater chance of choosing what is truly satisfying, rather than simply getting away from your present discontent. This is not easy to do. One way to make sure a new position provides more than just an escape is to carefully assess its potential for advancing you along your career path.

Creating Your Own Career Path

In this age of diversity, it would be a mistake to think that there is only one type of career path available. There are at least three that I think are reasonable alternatives in today's marketplace.

The first I call the *stable path*. It is taken by those who invest a great deal of time, energy, and money in becoming expert in a certain area and operating at a high, consistent level for life. The advantage of this path is that one is clear about what one has to do to succeed, almost from the start.

On the stable path, consistency assures success. The disadvantage is that someone on this path often has so much invested in their current career that changing seems almost impossible. I have a friend who, at thirty-two, had established himself as an excellent pathologist, well liked by both his patients and other physicians. One day, he confided that he was bored with his profession. He knew that all he needed to do to remain successful was be consistent and keep up with new research findings. Although he's had fantasies of changing fields, the thought of giving up everything he's achieved through the years boggles his mind. In his own way, he is in danger of getting ZAPped.

Another path is called the *climbing path*, after the proverbial ladder to climb. Someone on this course identifies an ultimate position as a goal, whether it is becoming president of a company, chief administrator of an agency, or tenured professor at a university, and outlines the steps needed to reach it. The advantage of the climbing path is that one can often identify the precise steps toward a certain result and then needs to master only a relatively narrow range of skills and expertise in order to take those steps. One disadvantage is that someone on the climbing path often limits the range of mastery in order to avoid diverting energy and in the process misses opportunities for moving up. Another disadvantage is simply that today there aren't enough ladders, and ultimately some will be left on the lower rungs.

The third path, and the one most likely to be considered by the majority of people reading this book, is the *expansive path*. Those on this route have realized or chosen to believe that a reasonable alternative to the stable path and climbing path is the development of a wide repertoire of skills that can be used in a variety of settings. The expansive path taker realizes that in today's marketplace:

**You don't need to be a specialist
or a generalist;
you need to be both.**

Those who choose the expansive path have many advantages. First, because one's skills are developed in a broad context, and are usable in an unlimited number of arenas, boredom becomes impossible. When, or if, it starts to set in, someone on this path need only move on, thus avoiding the traps of the stable path. The expansive path also has advantages over the climbing path, which tends to be rather narrow.

Because those on the expansive path sometimes lack the expertise for a particular job, they see some jobs as bridges to work requiring a higher level of expertise. Since the expansive path allows you to use a bridge rather than a ladder as a vehicle, you are never in danger.

**It's a lot easier to build a bridge
than to create a career ladder.**

For example, I recently worked with a client who had spent his life as an educator. On a climbing path, he set a goal of becoming a dean at an exclusive prep school. Having reached the top of his ladder at age forty, he experienced a crisis when he realized that he no longer wanted to work with kids. (Talk about getting ZAPped!)

He had two choices: to accept his fate and settle for twenty years of mediocrity, or to shift his concept of his career from climber to expander. Fortunately, he chose the latter (pun intended) and began to examine his strengths. Finally, he identified an area that he had done well in throughout his career and still liked: raising money. He chose to become either a development officer for a college or a professional fund-raising consultant. Like many expanders, he did not yet have what it would take to move into such a position right away; he decided he needed more experience. Eventually, he took what I call a "bridge job"—a job that will provide you with the experience to get the job you really want. Ideally, a bridge job is likable enough—so you don't feel tempted to jump off—but is really temporary and lasts only long enough to give you the experience you need to be really competitive in your field of choice. In this client's case, he got a job as director of a nonprofit charitable organization. They were happy to get someone with such impressive credentials, and he is now in position to prove his fund-raising powers and enter his new arena as an experienced competitor.

I'm not suggesting that everyone become an expander. We certainly need people who commit their lives to mastering critical fields. We also need people who commit themselves to their organizations and come to know them well enough over time to lead effectively. I am merely suggesting that for an increasing number of people, these old models don't fit and need to be abandoned in favor of the expansive path. Demographic data (e.g., baby boomers, shrinking middle management, numbers of people in law school) suggest that many will be forced to adopt this expansive notion. Why not do it intentionally?

Cutting a Deal: Negotiating for What You Want

When it comes to salary negotiation, a number of factors can prevent you from getting the best deal: doubts about your own worth, lack of information about what's possible, fear of losing a good offer, a general distaste for the process, or just being caught off guard. I worked with a manager who had recently switched companies. His old company went out of business, and the new one looked like a promising, growing young company. Excited about avoiding unemployment and getting in on the ground floor, he hadn't thought much about negotiating his salary. His interviewer asked what he was making at his last job and when he replied, the interviewer immediately said, "We can pay you that." Case closed. What could have been the beginning of a fruitful negotiation was now signed, sealed, and delivered. Had this manager been prepared for the inevitable salary question, he could have opened rather than shut the door to increased prosperity.

When I was traveling in the Middle East, one of the things

that struck me about the culture was the amount and nature of negotiating that goes on every day. I remember being in a shoe store and watching a customer and a clerk arguing over the price of a pair of shoes. In the end, the customer got his price. What is significant here is how willingly both parties entered into the negotiation. Imagine walking into your local shoe store with the same idea in mind. You would most likely be laughed out of the store, feeling even more foolish than when you walked in.

Because of many cultural norms, most Americans feel somewhat uncomfortable talking about money, particularly when it comes to such a personal thing as livelihood. Much of the time, this is not a problem. However, it can definitely be a handicap for the individual in need of negotiating a reasonable income.

Because most people dislike the salary negotiation phase of the job search, they often end up with significantly less money than they could have. Several myths about money help to perpetuate poor salary negotiation.

The Six Myths of Salary Negotiation (and the Realities)

Myth 1: It's rude and unwise to ask for too much money.

Myth 2: You could blow the offer if you push too hard.

Myth 3: Their first offer is usually their best offer.

Myth 4: The salary for most jobs is not negotiable.

Myth 5: When changing fields, you can't expect much money.

Myth 6: It's easier to ask for a raise once you've proven yourself than to go for a high initial salary.

Belief in any one of these myths can lead you to the low end of the salary range. To do your best in negotiation, you need to debunk these myths and any others you may carry with you that prevent you from getting what you're worth. Taking a look at the flip side of these myths will help you approach the negotiation process from a more powerful position.

Reality 1

Asking for what you are worth is neither rude nor unwise. The rudeness or lack of wisdom comes in the presentation. Bringing up the money issue before you have a clear idea of what the job involves is presenting your position when you're most vulnerable. Wait until you have an offer, or at least an idea of what they want from you. Once they know a little about you and you know a little about them, you're in a much better position to negotiate. Generally, the person doing the hiring will open the negotiations by bringing up the money issue. This is a perfect opportunity to ask them if they are making an offer. Once this is clear, it's time to make your best pitch. Keep in mind that if they've decided they want you, they probably have a lot invested in getting you and will be flexible in what they're willing to pay.

Reality 2

Many people are prevented from being hard-nosed salary negotiators by the fear that if they come on too strong, the other party will lose interest. This is simply not the case. The only way to get an offer rescinded as a result of the negotiation phase is to ask for a figure so ridiculous (too high or too low) that you convince the potential employer that you're a poor match for the job. Knowing the range of possibilities beforehand can remedy this problem. As long as you're negotiating for a figure that you know they can live with, go for the top of the range. When all is said and done, you'll be glad you did.

Reality 3

Assuming a first offer is the best offer is a convenient way for those of you who would just as soon not negotiate to rationalize saying yes prematurely. Unless you're dealing with a government job that has a specific figure written in stone, there is always room for negotiation. It is also safe to assume that regardless of the nobility of your prospective employer, the first figure is a low figure. If you're worth top dollar—and I'm assuming you are—you should realize that you won't be getting it unless you're willing to haggle a bit.

Reality 4

It is very easy to believe that the initial salary offer is a fixed figure, especially if the offer comes from a large, bureaucratic organization. Indeed, some organizations foster this impression, trying to reel you in at the least cost possible. It is up to you to put up a fuss. If you don't, you'll please your potential employer. But you'll also find yourself with less money than you could have had, perhaps less money than peers doing comparable work, and you will end up wishing you had pushed a little harder.

Reality 5

If you're changing careers, you are in an extremely vulnerable position during salary negotiation. Chances are your interviewer sees you as a potentially inexpensive catch who will be grateful just for the offer. The worst thing you can do is confirm this belief by showing your delight at getting an offer. The fact that you haven't worked in that field before is no reason for either of you to assume that you won't be able to contribute at a high level. In fact, you may be more valuable than some other employees because of the range of your experiences. You should use this selling point when someone makes an issue of your being new to the field.

My favorite story along these lines comes from a woman who went from an $18,000-a-year teaching job to a $40,000-a-year corporate training job. When the interviewer asked her what she made at her last job, she responded, "Not enough. That's why I'm here." She eventually got an offer at the top of that company's range.

When negotiating in a new field, remember that you have something to offer them that they want and that most other applicants for the position don't have. Don't let being new to the field work against you. Use it to your advantage and you'll get results.

Reality 6

The best time to get a raise is before you start the job. Many people will accept an offer they're not really satisfied with, thinking they will improve things once they're on board. That can happen occasionally, but generally it's much harder to move your salary up once it has been established. That initial salary will probably always be your base within the organization, even if you find you're making less than colleagues doing similar work. Chances are your increments will be much like everyone else's unless you change positions.

The tendency to get locked into a salary range is best illustrated by the case of a woman I know who works in insurance. She started her career as an underwriter in a large division. Over several years, she established herself as a highly professional and competent employee, so much so that she eventually became a supervisor of several other underwriters. One day, she was talking with a good friend who had similar responsibilities, but who had entered the organization at the supervisory level. She was amazed to find that her friend was making a substantially higher salary. When she went to her boss to discuss the inequity, she was told that nothing could be done. Subsequent efforts to get an upgrade were futile, and she realized that the only way to get what she was worth was to leave the company and enter another one as a supervisor.

In most organizations (though there are exceptions), people are categorized on the basis of their entrée to the point where making substantial jumps in salary, even highly warranted ones, becomes unlikely. The time to make your move is on your way in, when you still have some leverage and they're still not sure they have you. In fact, the allure of getting someone who costs a lot can work in your favor during salary negotiations. Once you've moved in, the allure is gone; you're just one of the gang. Although you need to take care not to be too hard to get, taking advantage of your position as a valuable commodity to be won *is* fair play. Chances are it's the last time you'll be in that position in that organization.

Paying attention to the subtle and not so subtle aspects of signing up is not always easy. All too often, people are swept away by the prospect of doing something new and different. Being close to getting a new job is an exciting, often frightening time. You need to call on all your resources, summon your intuitive powers, and utilize your problem-solving skills to make a sound decision. Pay attention to both your feelings and your thoughts, balance logic and intuition, maintain your perspective, and remember that *no* job is the only job. If you do all this, things will work out for the best.

EIGHT

—

Building a Base

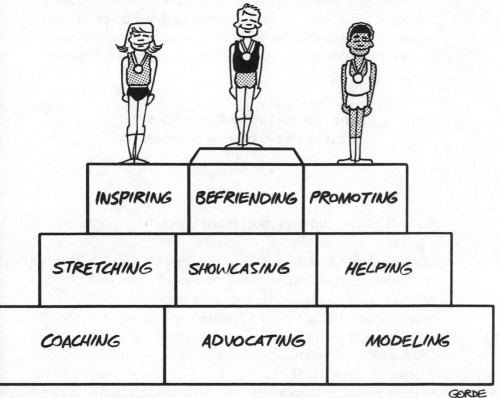

INSPIRING BEFRIENDING PROMOTING

STRETCHING SHOWCASING HELPING

COACHING ADVOCATING MODELING

GORDE

The Only Real Security

INDUSTRIAL PSYCHOLOGIST Harry Levinson stirred up a commotion recently when he suggested that anyone loyal to a company in today's volatile marketplace was a fool. Companies, he suggested, are not in the position to offer loyalty in return, nor are they necessarily able to reward loyalty received. Levinson was not suggesting that you be uncommitted to your organization and the work you do. He meant that you shouldn't assume you'll receive job security in return for good work.

The only real security you have is in what you have to offer an employer.

Gary S.: Banking on Good Hard Work

Gary S. worked for a small bank in New England, where he rose through the ranks from teller to loan officer and eventually to branch manager. He was an independent person who took pride in the fact that he "leaned on" no one to get to his current position. He believed—and demonstrated—that good hard work is all you need to get ahead.

His colleagues in the banking community made it a habit to keep on top of the various mergers and buyouts that were occurring increasingly, it seemed, throughout the region. One day, at one of the region's bank association meetings, several of these colleagues alerted him that a major international bank was buying up many of the small operations in the area. They wanted him to be aware that his bank seemed to fit the profile targeted by the corporate raiders. Gary laughed off their concern as hysteria and went about his business.

About two months later, Gary's colleagues' prophecy came true; his bank was bought by an international conglomerate. Shortly after the buyout, Gary was notified that his services were no longer needed. The new owners claimed they already had an excess of managers on their payroll.

What happened to Gary is happening to people in all walks of life all over the country. It is not an isolated case of a big, heartless corporation abusing poor, small-town businesses. It is an economic fact of life, and it is here to stay. Now, you may say there was nothing Gary could have done, that his fate was sealed. I beg to differ. Although Gary probably could not have prevented the takeover, he could have taken more responsibility for his own welfare, rather than relying on the paternal graces of his company. If he had, he might have been able to survive the takeover or to make a move before he was let go.

**The corporate patriarchy is
disappearing, and the
children need to fend for themselves.**

The nature of the global economy is such that whether they want to or not, companies are no longer able to protect the interests of their employees. If you can't rely on your company to take care of your career needs, who can you call on for help? The answer is simple: other people.

Mentoring in an Uncertain World

The term *mentoring* has many meanings. Its origins can be found in Homer's *Odyssey*. Mentor was a friend of King Ulysses, and during Ulysses' absence, he nurtured, protected, and educated Ulysses' son Telemachus. Mentor also helped Telemachus negotiate the world around him, introduced him to other leaders, and helped him find his rightful place in society.

Since then, the word has been used to describe everything from the old-boy network to a complex, high-level intimacy that defies definition. This chapter covers a range of activities that will help you develop mentoring relationships in order to achieve your goals and thrive in an increasingly volatile marketplace.

Mentoring is an elusive concept. I believe that you will be better served if, rather than try to define or describe it, I talk about the things that people in mentoring relationships do.

It is helpful to think about two types of mentoring activities: those that improve your performance and those that enhance your personal development. I call these *performance mentoring activities* and *personal mentoring activities*. You need the performance activities to help you do a better job and develop your competencies and the personal ones to bring you visibility and motivate you to do your best. In elaborating on each of the activities, I will give you an example of how that activity can work for you and will present some guidelines on how to act as either party in the relationship.

At this point, you may be saying to yourself, "Why is he telling me about both parties? I don't want to be a mentor; I just want to get mentored." First, I'd like to point out that no one "gets mentored." Daniel Levinson, author of *Seasons of a Man's Life* and probably the country's foremost expert on mentoring, suggests that many people misunderstand the concept. It's not, he suggests, like getting a computer or a raise. Real mentoring is much more subtle and complex and consequently more valuable. In addition, you really need to know both sides of the story.

The reason you should know both sides is best illustrated by a wonderful Japanese film, shot in Mongolia, called *Dersu Uzala*. It's full of profound lessons. A small mountain man named Dersu befriends a group of soldiers on a mission through the forest. The captain of the group and Dersu become good friends. The conditions are harsh, and food is scarce. After setting camp for the night Dersu and some of the soldiers gather food for the group. They eat heartily and have a good night's sleep. In the morning, each man packs his bag with rations and prepares to continue on his difficult journey. While the other men attend to their own needs, Dersu busily gathers the surplus food and prepares it for storage in the primitive hut they had hastily designed. Curious about Dersu's actions, the captain, with the other men looking on, asks what he's doing. Dersu replies, "Preparing the food for those who come after us." Puzzled, the captain asks, "Who do you think will come by?" Amused by his friend's obvious lack of understanding, Dersu answers, "Someone who needs food."

The sort of moving in the world represented by Dersu in this scene provides many lessons, one of which has to do with empowering oneself through the providing for others. Dersu is already powerful in the eyes of the soldiers as a result of his knowledge of and competence in the forest. This simple act, performed in a matter-of-fact way, further establishes him as a person of value.

In an age when organizational commitment is increasingly elusive, the only actions likely to reap rewards of loyalty and commitment are those that foster genuine respect and admiration. Dersu's motive was not to ensure that he would continue to be employed by the soldiers; his purpose was much deeper and more personal. Yet his actions resulted in his colleagues viewing him as an indispensable member of the group.

Providing services such as mentoring for others simply because you have the resources will establish you among co-workers as a person worthy of their association. Your actions will be rewarded in many ways.

Performance Mentoring Activities

Performance mentoring activities are those in which one person plays a consistent role in improving another person's performance. Although these relationships can exist in any area of life, research indicates that they occur most often in the workplace.

Coaching

One of the most basic mentoring activities is coaching. The most obvious examples of this activity are the roles coaches play in sports, dance, and drama. Take a moment to think about a great coach you've seen in public life—perhaps a football, baseball, or basketball figure, one of the great Olympic trainers, or a great acting teacher. If you figure out what it was about these people that made them great, you'll have the essence of coaching.

Take, for example, the late choreographer, Bob Fosse. In recent years, you've probably learned more about Fosse's personal habits than you care to know. However, the barrage of information about him, the autobiographical film *All That Jazz*, and the postmortem ramblings that accompany the death of any well-known figure have shed some light on his masterful coaching ability. When you hear the name *Fosse*, you immediately think of the unmistakable dance steps he created. People who would not recognize the man if they saw him on the street would probably recognize (if they'd seen any of his work) any dance pieces that he choreographed. Compare this with, say, Baryshnikov, who is much more the dancer than the coach, and you'll see how the recognition factor changes significantly.

Great coaching is not always found in the same place as great performance. What made Bob Fosse great was not his dancing ability but his ability to convey his creative vision through the actions of others, to teach other dancers to dance magnificently. This is the essence of coaching: to teach others to be masterful. It can be found in the most unlikely places.

Strategies for Coaching

The key to effective coaching is to match a person who has certain knowledge and skills to convey and the ability and desire to convey them with someone who has the need and desire to learn that knowledge and those skills.

For the Mentored

I like, as you may have already noticed, to debunk truisms that contain more falsity than truth. For example:

Those who cannot do, teach.

This belief can be the kiss of death for you when searching for a strong coaching relationship. Doing and coaching are particular abilities that require very different skills, interests, and motivations. If you're looking for a coach, the last place to look is in someone who is at the peak of his or her career. These people are probably too busy fostering their own success to pay much attention to yours.

Let's go back to sports for a moment. How often do you see a player at the peak of his or her career spending time developing others? (The occasional awe-inspiring player-coach is the exception.) Most athletic coaches have played in the past but are no longer active in the field. The truly great coaches are the ones who have become expert strategists, with insight into the strengths and limitations of each player and the ability to see the whole picture.

If you want a good coach, find someone who has these abilities, and—this is important—seems particularly interested in helping *you*.

For the Mentor

I meet many people who, after success in a variety of endeavors, find themselves lost at forty, fifty, or sixty. Now that they've proved themselves, they feel there's nothing left to accomplish. Most of these people eventually react in one of three ways: They realize that they need the charge of proving themselves again and find new challenges; they decide that now that the burden of proving themselves is gone, the challenge is to find something to do that is fun; or they find that what they really want to do is share what they've learned with others, thereby leaving a legacy.

Those of you who find yourselves in the third group are the ones I'm speaking to here. Whatever your field, your organization, or your position, coaching can be the vehicle for ensuring immortality in your life's work. Developing someone by sharing your knowledge of the tricks of the trade, honing their skills, and increasing their mastery of the field can provide the deep satisfaction you crave. Through coaching, you can perform a unique role in a developing professional's life by providing the perspective that you alone, as a seasoned professional, have to offer. Use your coaching abilities freely and carefully. You will be richly rewarded.

Stretching

An interesting and sometimes confusing performance mentoring activity is *stretching*. Stretching involves identifying an area in which someone needs to grow in order to enhance their performance and creating conditions that foster this growth. The tricky thing about stretching is that the mentored person often will not realize the benefits of the experience until after the fact.

Do It Again

During my junior year in college, I had the good fortune to be instructed—and stretched—by Dr. Mary Louise Fowler. The course was Advanced Composition, and this was Dr. Fowler's last year of teaching. She approached the task of teaching writing with a stern determination that most of us attributed to her being on the edge of retirement. The class involved writing papers on a variety of topics and using a variety of approaches. After each assignment, Dr. Fowler would return papers; and if she felt there was room for improvement, she would demand a rewrite. I never produced a paper that she didn't ask me to rewrite. In fact, I received a barrage of C grades from her, often for papers rewritten four or five times. I was so frustrated by her familiar "Do it again!" on the top of every paper that I often considered dropping the class. It wasn't until the end of the term, when I received an A in the course, that I realized I was not being labeled average by Dr. Fowler but was being developed to what she saw as my full potential. My gratitude for her stretching and its impact on my career is greatest now, fifteen years later, as I write this book.

**Find people who are willing to give you a
hard time, and let them.**

Strategies for Stretching

The key to an effective stretching relationship is to identify a certain aspect of a person's potential and then work to develop it. Most often, such relationships are fueled by a creative tension between the two people and are based on one party's willingness to challenge the other and the other's willingness to be challenged.

For the Mentored

As my story demonstrates, it's often only in retrospect that a person realizes he or she has been stretched. Therefore, there may be times when you feel you're being treated unfairly when you are really being challenged to excel.

> **Before you accuse someone of being on
> your case, consider carefully that
> they might be on your side.**

The next time you feel challenged, don't assume the challenger is your enemy. He or she may be a valuable ally. Accept the challenge, and watch for results. You may be glad you did.

For the Mentor

Seeing potential in people beyond what they see in themselves is a gift. Use it as often as you can, and the rewards will be great. But a word of caution is in order: If you're really stretching someone, you may be in for some hostility. Being stretched is never comfortable. Be sure you choose someone who is trustworthy and likely to appreciate the stretching in the long run. Choose your stretching partner carefully, and you'll find that:

> **If they don't like what you're doing,
> they'll probably be glad you did it.**

Paradoxical as this may seem, the more painful the stretching, the more valuable the stretch. Be prepared to tolerate the strain if you think the results will be worthwhile.

Modeling

I am going to tell you a story that illustrates the power of modeling by painting a picture of what effective modeling is *not*.

A long time ago, I worked for an agency that specialized in

helping troubled teenagers. One summer, four of us took twelve of these young people camping for three days. The trip was intended to teach them about leadership. Our senior staff member was the director of the agency and a likable guy, but he was not known for his industriousness. When we arrived at the campground, each of us went to work. One person gathered firewood; another unloaded supplies for dinner; I began pitching tents. As we engaged our adolescent charges in the various chores, we noticed the director busily setting up his hammock. A few minutes later, he got in the hammock, lay back, and proceeded to read a book aptly titled *Mismanagement in the Human Service Agency.*

This brief and, if you were there, poignant story illustrates two important points: First, you never forget your models, good or bad. Second, you can learn a great deal by studying the beliefs, attitudes, and behaviors of people in powerful positions. For example, by keeping in mind my director's shortsightedness, lack of consideration, and blindness to his impact on his subordinates (we were all furious), I have avoided making the same mistakes in my working life.

Although a negative model can powerfully demonstrate how not to be, the positive models we choose to emulate are even more powerful.

I'd like you to spend a few minutes completing the next two-part activity, in which I ask you to identify three people you might think of as heroes. Don't let the word throw you. Heroes don't have to be perfect. For example, you may at first think of JFK as a hero for his handling of the Cuban missle crisis but then hesitate to list him because of recent speculation on the impropriety of his personal activities. In this case, I would encourage you to list him for the heroic aspects and leave the rest for some other time. In other words, think of aspects of people that you admire, even if you don't buy the whole package. If the word *heroes* still bothers you, try substituting *model*. Once you've completed the first part, list the characteristics of those three heroes (or models) that you would most like to emulate.

Profile on Heroic Models

FLESH AND BLOOD HERO (mentor, advisor, manager, etc.)	CELLULOID HERO (film, fantasy, comic book character, etc.)	FAMOUS HERO (political, religious, professional, sports, or other public figure)
Name	Name	Name

CHARACTERISTICS OF IDENTIFIED HEROES

(phrases that describe their actions, values, beliefs, etc.)

1. _____	1. _____	1. _____
2. _____	2. _____	2. _____
3. _____	3. _____	3. _____
4. _____	4. _____	4. _____
5. _____	5. _____	5. _____
6. _____	6. _____	6. _____
7. _____	7. _____	7. _____
8. _____	8. _____	8. _____
9. _____	9. _____	9. _____
10. _____	10. _____	10. _____

Personal Heroic Profile

Using the data from your profile of heroic models, list the ten characteristics from the three identified heroes that you would most like to emulate.

1. _____
2. _____
3. _____
4. _____
5. _____

6. _____

7. _____

8. _____

9. _____

10. _____

What you now have is a blueprint or prototype for the kind of people you would like to model. If you examine the way people become masterful, you will see that they often study people who do things well and replicate their patterns.

I call this *intentional modeling* because whether they know it or not, everybody models behavior. Since much (some would argue all) behavior is learned, it makes sense that people model other people. The notions that you parent the way you were parented, teach the way you were taught, or manage the way you were managed echo this belief. If this is true, why not choose those models you want to pattern yourself after rather than leave it to chance or "good genes."

Review the models and the attributes you chose, and begin seeking out people in your world who most clearly reflect those qualities. You will soon find yourself leaping toward your self-determined potential.

Nondirective Helping

This mentoring role is based on the work of the late psychologist Carl Rogers and consists of developing a problem-solving relationship with someone who doesn't solve your problems but helps *you* solve them. Rather than offer advice, guidance, or solutions, nondirective helpers act as mirrors, reflecting your thoughts about your dilemma. They get you to focus your own energy and resources. Good listeners make good nondirective helpers. Their investment is in helping you understand your perspective and moving you toward solutions of your own design.

**Nondirective helping is harder
than you think.**

As a career counselor, I am often confronted with people who want me to tell them what to do. Occasionally, I oblige; but more often, I try to help them in a nondirective fashion. I used to think this was easier than giving advice, but I now know it's much harder. It's much easier to present your opinion than to help others clarify their own.

**Good listeners help people
hear themselves.**

Trudy: The Horrifying Life of a High School Teacher

Trudy had been a high school teacher for twelve years. She came to see me for an individual consultation during the course of a workshop series. She told me she had decided to shift into the corporate sector and work in personnel. Her dilemma was whether to keep her teaching job while looking for personnel work. Here is an excerpt of our conversation.

T.: I've decided to definitely leave teaching and go into personnel.

N.Y.: Great, what can I do for you?

T.: Well, I'm not sure whether to quit my job or wait until I have a new one first.

N.Y.: Uh-huh.

T.: I've heard it's harder to get a job if you don't have one. Is that true?

N.Y.: That seems to be the case.

T.: Maybe I should stay until I find something else. I think that would be safer.

N.Y.: Sounds like you'd rather play it safe than risk the unknown.

T.: The thought of not having a job does scare me.

N.Y.: What does the thought of going back to the teaching job next fall do?

T.: It horrifies me! I think I'll hand in my resignation. Thanks for helping me figure things out.

Trudy made her decision completely on her own, yet she thought I helped her do it. In fact, all I did was help her to think about her own need to make a decision. She did the rest. She probably would have made the same decision on her own, but having someone to mirror her thoughts quickened the process.

On Recognizing a Nondirective Helper

They're not the people who say, "Let me give you a good piece of solid advice."

Finding someone to give you advice is easy; finding someone who will listen to you is much harder. You know you've found a good, nondirective helper when you walk away from a conversation feeling you were heard and understood. If your conversations with this person led you, not to a change of view, but to clarification of what you had already been thinking, you know you're on the right track.

The payoff for nondirective helpers comes from the process of helping you solve your problems, not from getting you to see things their way. They are not the people with whom you engage in power struggles or argue. They are invested less in what you decide to do and more in how you go about deciding. They appreciate process as well as content, form as well as substance. Their primary concern is as a developer of your problem-solving abilities. Treat them carefully; they are a rare find.

On Being a Nondirective Helper

Choose and use this role carefully. Many people, upon learning how to be a nondirective helper, become overzealous and use their skills inappropriately. For example:

A: I wonder what's for lunch. I'm starved.
B: Sounds like you're feeling hungry.

Telling someone something they already know is not what nondirective helping is all about. Helping someone explore all the subtle ramifications of a particular decision is more to the point. Examining options with someone without stating your opinion is not an easy thing for Americans to do. We are highly opinionated about almost everything. This is fine when you are invested in the answer to a particular problem. Another type of investment, however, has to do with developing people around you who can think for themselves. Nondirective helping empowers them by helping them to help themselves. By providing such opportunities, you'll be helping others refine their own problem-solving abilities, and you'll be surprised at how much you learn in the process.

Personal Mentoring Activities

Whereas performance mentoring activities focus on enhancing your career by improving your performance on the job, personal mentoring activities affect your career movement more directly. Finding people within and beyond your organization who will help you attain and maintain a strong position in the marketplace is what these activities are all about.

Promoting

Promoting involves establishing relationships with people who value your worth enough to advance your career whenever the opportunity emerges. When they hear the word *promoting*, most people think of it in the most literal sense, as something a boss might do (i.e., give you a promotion). But promoting as a personal mentoring activity involves much more.

Earlier in this book, I talked about the information age and the fact that people now gather information insatiably. The more they get, the better. Besides having an impact on almost every other aspect of contemporary life, this phenomenon has direct consequences for your career advancement. In this information age, if the person considering you for a job, transfer, project, or assignment has never heard of you before, chances are slim that they will hire you. With the flood of information bombarding people every day comes the expectation that if something (or someone) is of value to them, they would have heard already.

It's true that a certain amount of self-promotion is critical to your career success, but the notion that you can do it all, amid the vast, ever-changing global data bank, is unrealistic. You need help. Engaging in mentoring relationships with people who are willing and able to promote you is one way to speed and increase the likelihood of your success.

Strategies for Promoting

You can't make someone promote you. In fact:

**You can lead a horse to water, but if
you're not careful, he'll run for the desert.**

Promoting is one of the most sensitive of the mentoring activities. Nothing turns a promoter off faster than pressure to promote. Let's go back to the literal aspect of promotion for an illustration.

Gerry T.: The Promotion Principle

Gerry T. was a supervisor for a small graphic design firm. During his three years with the firm, Gerry had successfully managed four different accounts and had lured two major accounts away from other firms. For several months, he had been thinking about approaching his boss for a raise and a promotion, but he felt he wasn't ready to give it his best shot. One weekend, Gerry attended a design convention where he showed several people his work. On the last day of the show, he received an attractive offer with a firm in a distant state. Though he didn't want to move, Gerry decided this was the leverage he had been waiting for. On Monday morning, he went in and asked for his raise and promotion. He began by telling his boss of his new offer. His boss congratulated him and suggested that if it was indeed as good as it sounded, he should accept it. He added, finally, that Gerry would be missed if he decided to go.

Gerry's biggest mistake was posing his request in the form of a threat, violating what I call the *promotion principle*:

**Don't tell them what they have to lose
by not promoting you.
Tell them what they have to gain
by promoting you.**

I don't know about you, but I don't like to be threatened. I'm not suggesting that Gerry should have hidden the fact that he received a good offer, only that he should have started with the positive. He should have reminded his boss of the successes he's had, what he was doing now, and what he planned to do next for the company, pointing out that he could continue his good work with more support (i.e., money and status). Now let's generalize about the type of promotion that is less concrete, but equally important: word-of-mouth promotion.

For the Mentored

Good word-of-mouth promotion can create opportunities that a low profile can never generate. I'm not suggesting that everyone go out and sing their own praises all the time; some people are just not cut out for that. But if you can get someone else to sing them for you, your options will increase dramatically. When I first started doing career workshops about seven years ago, I had a hard time selling them. The topic is a difficult one to face, and no one had heard of me. I had to use every promotional tool in the book—radio, TV, public speaking, newspapers, freebies, brochures, the works—to get even a minimum number of participants. As my clientele grew, I changed my strategy. Now I maintain a mailing list of past participants and write them every two months, sending a few brochures and asking them to spread the word. That's all I have to do to fill a group. In other words, my clients or customers have become my primary promoters.

There's one other thing I do. Sociologist Robert Cialdini has written a book called *Influence,* in which he talks about the concept of reciprocation. We have all experienced the phenomenon; it has to do with the drive to do things for people who do things for you. That's why the vacuum cleaner salesman gives you a "treasure chest of free gifts" when he arrives. He hopes it will compel you to do something for him—buy the machine.

I keep this principle in mind when I write my broadcasting request letter to my alumni. I often include information I think may be helpful and an invitation to call me if they're having trouble. Now some of you may be thinking, "What a manipulator!" But there's a difference between manipulation and getting yourself some invaluable promotion. There is nothing wrong with honestly offering people something they can use and openly asking for something in return or genuinely giving someone something of value that compels them to return the favor. When I make my offer to help, I mean it; and some people take me up on it.

If you don't make your needs known to people who are likely to help you, you won't get the visibility you need in today's chaotic marketplace. The key is making honest requests in an honest fashion.

For the Mentor

With the power that promotion holds comes the ability to influence. I recently observed two incidents of the power of negative promotion in the information-crazed culture that is so much a part of contemporary life. They demonstrate the need to treat promotion carefully.

While I was shopping for a printer for my new computer, I overheard the salesman talking about one of his lines of clones. The customer said, "I was told to stay away from them." When asked why, he said, "I don't know, but that's what I was told." And he walked out. The salesman, not sure what to do, stood there scratching his head. I, in turn, walked out of the store, thinking I'd better stay away from the brand—and I have no idea why.

That same evening, I overheard a drugstore clerk tell a customer that one of the local restaurants was forced to fire seven of its evening staff for illicit drug use on the job. I don't know if that's true or not, but I found myself thinking as I passed the restaurant that it will be a while before I eat there again.

We are bombarded with more information than we have time to process. Some of this information slips into our consciousness through the back door and influences our behavior. All this suggests that each of you has the power to promote others. The more people who trust you and the greater the trust, the more influential you can be. It is worth your while, and truly worthwhile to those you promote and those to whom you promote them, to be careful and clear about what you know and what you say. Offering good information about people's good work will help everyone in the long run.

Showcasing

Showcasing involves finding people who have the power and willingness to expose you to others in a way that enhances your career. Because the ability to showcase someone depends on one's power, it is one of the mentoring activities most likely to occur exclusively between superiors and subordinates. There may be many motives involved, including a belief in a person's abilities, a desire to promote one's own people, or an interest in competing with other units, divisions, or organizations. But whatever the motive, finding yourself the object of someone's showcasing interest can enhance your career tremendously.

Ron B.: From Studio Manager to World Traveler

Ron B. was manager of a TV studio at a small community college. He was very talented but not particularly ambitious. The president of the college, who was very interested in emerging technologies, noticed Ron had done some good work on recent grants, creating interesting interactive videos. The president decided to showcase Ron's talents. He began bringing local corporate executives, touring business people, and visiting legislators into the studio whenever the opportunity arose. They were always introduced to Ron and shown samples of his innovative work. During this time, the president also encouraged Ron to develop new ideas. Eventually, Ron began getting all sorts of offers, which the president encouraged him to accept. The best offer he got was to go overseas and manage the construction of a TV studio for a small developing country. He is now on leave from the college, doing work he never dreamed possible. Had he not been showcased, he'd still be in his little studio.

Strategies for Showcasing

Some of you may be thinking, "What a fool the president was! He lost one of his best people. That guy will never want to come back to his modest studio." You're right about the last part, but wrong about the rest. The president reaps several benefits from showcasing talented people the way he did: First, he gets people's best work when they're hungriest. Second, he establishes a reputation as a good person to work for, thus attracting other talented people. And third, he develops a broad network of successful and influential contacts. Consider the alternative. Ron, a creative, talented employee, would not have stayed with the college forever. What the president did was recognize talent and utilize it in the most fruitful way possible for all involved.

For the Mentored

As you read the story of Ron and the college president, you may think Ron was just lucky to have been chosen. Good fortune certainly played a part. But if you're looking to be showcased, there are several things you can do to better your chances. The first, perhaps the obvious, thing is to do high-quality work. All the politics in the world will not substitute for having the goods when it comes to being showcased. Next, be sure to let your desired showcaser know what you're up to and how it may benefit him or her. Finally, don't assume your immediate supervisor is the one with whom to work (but never cross your immediate boss unless you're ready to leave). Look up the organizational ladder to see if there's someone who might be particularly interested in what you do or how you do it. Ron's immediate supervisor was the academic dean, and although they got along well, the dean was not particularly interested in Ron's innovations. The president was, and Ron was able to maintain good relationships with both. If you can identify someone with power who's impressed enough with your abilities to showcase your talents, you may find yourself with opportunities you never before dreamed of.

For the Mentor

The best way to keep what you have
is to give it away.

There are several lessons for the mentor in Ron's preceding
story. The worst mistake a manager or supervisor can make
is to hold someone back for fear of losing their contribution.
As a supervisor, the choice is yours: You can develop a valuable contributor and risk that they will leave, or you can hold
them back and ensure their departure. The difference is that
when they leave because of growth, you've probably gotten
your money's worth. When they leave out of frustration, they
probably haven't been performing optimally for quite some
time.

There's another factor: When it comes to communication,
it is truly a small world. Someone who leaves your charge
because of growth will invariably attract more talented people
to your shop; someone who leaves because of lack of opportunity is the recruiter's kiss of death. Developing your
organization's reputation as a place where people can make
a contribution and move on to better things is one of the best
things you can do to ensure a quality pool of applicants for
filling crucial roles in the future.

Advocating

If you're going to take risks in your career, even careful ones,
there will be times when your strategies backfire. Having
someone on your side who's willing to support you, run inter-
ference for you, and protect you can make the difference between surviving a disaster and becoming a casualty. There is
a delicate balance between having too little and too much
advocacy: Too little can get you into trouble, and too much
can make you seem unable to take care of yourself.

Strategies for Advocating

Whichever side of the fence you're on, you want to be sure you understand which situations are appropriate for you to handle and which are better left to the other party. Good judgment and strong analytical skills are essential for this type of relationship to work.

For the Mentored

An advocate is probably the most difficult type of person to find. If you can find someone who really has your best interests in mind, you are truly fortunate. Having someone you can trust when you're most vulnerable means that you've established a relationship with someone who really cares about you. In accepting someone's advocacy on your behalf, be sure that you do indeed trust this person to represent your interests. Also, be aware that because an advocate comes to your aid during high-risk times, you may tend to feel indebted. Be sure your relationship with the advocate is based on mutual appreciation, not on the assumption that favors will be returned. Nothing is worse than feeling indebted to someone for saving your skin—except finding out that you are.

For the Mentor

Advocacy presents you with a unique opportunity. The more powerful you are, the more successful you've been, the more you have to give and to gain in the role of advocate. Advocacy provides an opportunity to use your subtle, refined aptitudes for managing delicate problems. Much of the work of senior professionals is straightforward, involving skills honed over time to a high level of efficiency. Advocating for a junior colleague in trouble gives you a chance to stretch yourself again and really make a contribution to your organization—and to the development of another human being. Saving someone you deem worthwhile from embarrassment or worse can make your years of juggling organizational dynamics seem worth it. You also need to be careful, though. If you're going to save someone's neck, be sure that they're worth saving and that the price you pay is worth it to you.

Inspiring

This mentoring activity differs from all the others in that it most likely occurs outside the workplace. Most people are too caught up in the day-to-day workings of their jobs to inspire others. That's why many organizations call on motivational speakers or consultants. People need that outside perspective to get inspired about what they do. But although organizations can inspire you to get work done, you need to look elsewhere for inspiration in managing your career.

Strategies for Gaining Inspiration

There are many sources of inspiration. The trick is finding one that helps you manage your career. Some people look to the spiritual for inspiration, finding what they need in a religious leader, gatherings or groups, or reading materials.

Books can be an excellent source of inspiration; some people call them paper mentors. When I was writing this book, I picked up *Unlimited Power* by Anthony Robbins. It was the perfect book for me at the perfect time because it is full of stories of people reaching their full potential, and strategies for achieving your own. It gave me the motivation to keep going when I needed it. There are many books in a range of categories that can do the same for you; I hope this book is one. For example, if you wanted a book that puts your concerns in perspective and demonstrates your ability to control your own destiny, you might pick up Norman Cousin's *Anatomy of an Illness,* in which he describes how he conquered a life-threatening disease by bombarding himself with a daily dose of laughter. If he could laugh his way back to health, perhaps you could learn how to laugh your way out of a work crisis or difficult job search.

Groups can be another source of inspiration. As I mentioned earlier, many of my career seminar participants form groups, after completing the seminars, to both support and inspire each other. The self-help movement in this country has spawned hundreds of types of groups, and many can provide you with inspiration to get you through a difficult period. They can help with such things as a difficult job search and problems related to a reorganization or a relationship with a boss. People often claim that having a group to share their problems with can make all the difference in the world.

The arts offer inspiration, too. Some people collect movies that feature characters, scenes, or plots they find inspirational. They watch these movies whenever they need an "inspiration fix." I think it's a great idea. Another arts-related approach involves music. In my workshops, I use music to get people to focus. (It works better for some people than for others.) I use songs like "Get a Job," and "Working on a Chain Gang" to get people to laugh and to think about their situations. You could create a tape with your favorite songs, maybe even work songs. But stay away from the depressing ones; stick to the uplifting ones. Listen to your tape whenever you need a shot in the arm. Some people like to listen to prerecorded motivational tapes; others prefer making personalized versions. The results can be quite powerful.

These are just a few ideas for inspiring yourself to do whatever it takes to move you forward in your career. There are many others. Pay attention to what and who inspires you, and spend time with that person or thing. Keep in mind:

Inspiration is the catalyst of change.

Friendship

Some people say it's better not to get too friendly with the people at work. Frankly, I think that's crazy. You spend half your waking hours at work and the other half taking care of your family, house, pets, boat, yard, aging parents, wardrobe, whatever. If you're like most of us, you don't have much time to spend on developing and nurturing friendships. Although being open to friendships at work is risky, the rewards far outweigh the risks.

I believe this issue is critical to the quality of your work life. The people I know who are truly happy with their work are the ones who like the people they work with. It doesn't matter whether your work involves other people or is primarily solitary. If you don't enjoy the people around you, you will not enjoy your work. I'm not suggesting you need to be close buddies with all your co-workers, only that you need at least one or two people in your environment whom you can trust. *Trust* is the key word here. True friendship is a relationship with someone you can really count on. The challenge is to find someone in your organization who will befriend you with no strings attached. Many of you may be reticent, having been burned by trusting the wrong people. The key to developing friendships at work is identifying people you are drawn to because you have something in common other than your work. This common bond may be music, fashion, sports, family, politics, hobbies, or something else. So long as the common link is not work-related, it can serve as a focus for the relationship. Although relationships among peers are generally less complicated, I've seen strong friendships exist between superiors and subordinates.

Robert T.: The New Wave in Underwriting

Robert T. had worked as an underwriter for a major insurance company for three years. He liked his job and believed he had a good future with the company, but he often felt isolated, as though he didn't fit in. Robert noticed that the norms of the organization were such that people did not talk about "outside things." One day, he overheard his boss, a middle-aged executive, on the phone ordering tickets for a Talking Heads concert. Not sure whether the tickets were for himself or his children, Robert didn't say anything. But when he went to the concert (Talking Heads was his favorite group), he kept an eye out for his boss. Sure enough, he spotted him down the aisle—with his wife but not his children. The next day, Robert mentioned the concert, and watched his boss' face light up. Eventually, he and his boss sat down and talked about their shared passion for new wave rock music. They now exchange tapes and occasionally go to concerts together. More important, their friendship has blossomed, extending into other aspects of their lives, including concern for each other's families and an overall interest in each other's well-being.

Relationships like this one are hard to come by, but the rewards of having someone at work who cares about you are worth the effort.

Strategies for Building Friendships at Work

The biggest problem with friendships at work is the ulterior motive. Nothing can contaminate a friendship faster than the realization that the other person is in it for the payoff. There are no separate guidelines here for the mentor and the mentored because for a friendship to work, the two people must meet on common ground.

Keeping in mind your current interests and values, look for people in your organization whose personal priorities seem to parallel yours. Find a creative way to let these people know you have a common interest and talk about it whenever you get the chance. Eventually, it will become clear whether you have a potential friend or just another passing acquaintance. The important thing is to build friendships when you're not desperate for them. When you are in need, it's often too late to find them.

Cross-Gender Mentoring Relationships

This issue is such a hot one that I hate to bring it up. However, it would be foolish to stay away from cross-gender relationships because by doing so, you automatically eliminate half the possibilities in a field that is already far too narrow. There are two concerns to keep in mind when engaging in cross-gender mentoring relationships. The first is attraction.

**Just because you're attracted
doesn't mean you're guilty.**

One strategy people use to cope with uncomfortable situations is to deny them. Such a situation can easily arise if you engage in any mentoring activities with someone of the opposite sex and become attracted to the other party. To a great extent, this is predictable and natural. If you are on either end of a relationship more intimate than a typical work relationship, it is reasonable that you may develop personal feelings that extend beyond roles. Whether we're talking about mentoring or not, it happens everyday. The challenge in a mentoring relationship is to not let the guilt associated with those feelings interfere with the development and maintenance of the relationship. On the other hand, if you *are* guilty, you need to come to terms with the potentially damaging impact of your actions on your career and the other person's. Some organizations are fairly tolerant of relationships between employees; others are not. Regardless, you need to tread carefully when on delicate ground. This is particularly true with cross-gender relationships because:

**Even if you're not guilty,
you might as well be.**

People outside mentoring relationships are often jealous of people inside them and sometimes look for ways to dis-

credit them. The cross-gender aspect of a mentoring relationship provides the perfect scenario for a jealous outsider.
Be assured that a meaningful relationship between opposite
sexes will invariably come under great scrutiny. Be clear
about your boundaries. Don't look for trouble. Don't compromise your own sense of propriety. Do these three things,
and you will ultimately be respected by the people who count.

Multiple Mentoring Relationships:
The Mentoring Mandala

**Mandala: a concentric organization of
geometric shapes; the wheel of life.**

Unless you are extraordinarily lucky, you probably won't have
all your mentoring needs met by one person or even by a few
people. Chances are you will need a group of people to provide you with a range of functions for advancing and thriving
in your career.

Getting Rolling

The Old Model

I'm going to talk about wheels for a while: old wheels, new
wheels, and life-affirming wheels. The old wheel is the organizational model you are all familiar with. It consists of the
organization as the hub and people as the various spokes.

One significant aspect of the old model is that the organization is the central element. The organization determines
what happens to the various players. Your behavior in relationship to the other players is influenced—shaped—by the
activities of the organization.

I talked earlier about the traditional role of the organization as protector of its people and the rapid demise of that

The Old Model

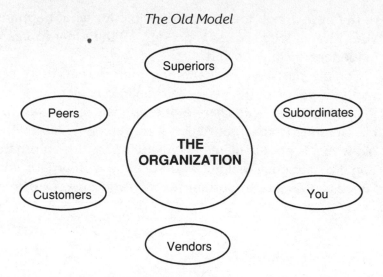

role. I also talked about the need for people to rethink their role in the organization in light of these changing relationships.

The New Model

The new model shifts the burdens and benefits of responsibility to you, whether you want them or not. You are the hub

The New Model

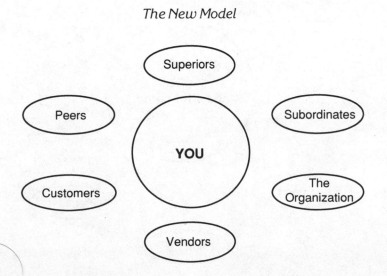

of the new wheel, the one responsible for what happens to you. The various spokes represent all the other forces that influence you in your work.

For the purposes of managing your career, think of the various spokes of the wheel as the various elements affecting your career. This change of emphasis shifts your frame of reference from organizational to personal. Although the old wheel is not obsolete, it is useful only from an organizational perspective, helpful when dealing with organizational success. It is less important for focusing on your own success.

The Great Mandala

There's one more wheel, and it has to do with increasing the quality of your life at work and creating conditions that will enable your career to soar. It takes its name from an old folk

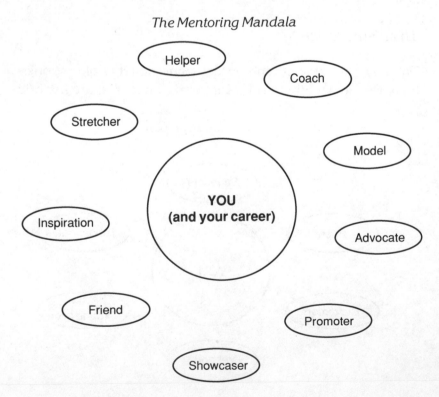

The Mentoring Mandala

song, "The Great Mandala," or wheel of life. To really thrive in your career, you need to develop a broad range of relationships (outlined in this chapter) that foster your development personally and professionally, within and beyond the parameters of your current job. The *mentoring mandala* is shown on page 220.

Your Mentoring Mandala

Your mentoring mandala forms a constellation of special people in your life who provide you with a variety of services designed to optimize your performance and your success. Although no one person can fulfill all your mentoring needs, some individuals may occupy several positions at once. Maintain yourself at the hub of your mandala, and keep the spokes of your wheel full. Your career will never be the same.

Your Mentoring Mandala

NINE

Staying on Top

Managing Your Career: "The Boss" Style

WHETHER YOU like his music or not, if you study the career of singer Bruce Springsteen, you will find that he has an uncanny ability to stay on top. I believe his nickname, "The Boss," is appropriate. He is an expert at career management, and much can be learned from observing his performance over the past fifteen years.

From the beginning, Springsteen demonstrated an ability to maintain his integrity in the face of overwhelming odds. His first two records, although critically acclaimed, were for the most part commercially unsuccessful because of the length of the songs and their "lack of accessibility." Although he was aware of the formula for success, Springsteen opted to follow his artistic inclination rather than compromise the quality of his work.

When he finally broke into the mainstream in 1975 with the landmark album *Born to Run*, Springsteen became the victim of media hype. He made the covers of both *Newsweek* and *Time* in the same week and was immediately labeled a media invention. Soon afterward, Springsteen became entangled in a legal battle that prevented him from recording for over three years, a dilemma that would have left someone less adept at managing his career with no career left to manage. In subsequent years, Springsteen released two albums that were well received but still lacked the formulaic properties associated with superstardom.

Just as he seemed ready to catapult to the top of mainstream popular music, he challenged the norm once again with his least accessible album, *Nebraska,* a collection of mournful folk songs in the tradition of Woody Guthrie.

One thing that has kept Springsteen a major figure throughout his career is that like all successful professionals, he does not rely on one skill alone. In addition to his ability to write and sing distinctive songs, he is a masterful performer. His concerts are legendary for their flawless delivery and commitment to excellence.

Following *Nebraska* came the record-breaking *Born in the U.S.A.,* which finally delivered Springsteen into a superstardom the likes of which few artists have experienced. After that came the long-anticipated five-record live album that set a new standard for the industry.

Next came the true test. After the staggering success of *Born in the U.S.A.* and the live set came speculation that Springsteen was trapped and could never meet the expectations of an increasingly demanding public. Once again, his mastery in managing his own career came through. Rather than attempt to top *Born in the U.S.A.*, Springsteen chose to release *Tunnel of Love* in 1987. This album was smaller in scope yet richer in texture than its predecessors, full of reflection and subtlety and requiring careful listening—hardly the stuff of which follow-up hit albums are made. Clearly, he realized the danger of becoming a caricature of himself, a danger all artists face at the peak of their careers. Springsteen's release of a soft, introspective album was proof of his ability to maintain the quality of his career and stay on top.

This discussion of Bruce Springsteen is not intended to impress you with my knowledge of pop music. What I want to impress upon you are several important considerations for staying on top in your career.

1. Be guided by your own best judgment, and follow your instincts. Successful career management involves a blend of common sense, persistence, appropriate timing, intuition, and integrity.
2. Develop more than one competency. You never know when circumstances will arise that prevent you from using your primary skill.
3. Apply the same standards of excellence to everything you do. Don't substitute quantity for quality.

4. Don't stagnate. Each major project you work on should develop you in some way. Otherwise, you're wasting precious time and creative potential.

5. Don't worry about criticism for not being consistent. Lack of consistency is often a sign of ingenuity. If what you're doing is of value, others will adjust.

6. Know when to give other people what they want, and give it freely.

7. Accept the fact that a crisis may provide opportunity as well as danger.

If you keep all these points in mind, you will find yourself in good position to stay on top in your career. There are many other things you can do to ensure that you don't fall from grace once you've achieved success. Those concerns will be addressed later in this chapter in "The Seven Sides of Every Organization" (page 231).

Skill Mastery: The Keystone of Your Success

Although we all can't experience the fame and fortune of a Bruce Springsteen, we can achieve our own success. Perhaps the most helpful contribution you can make to your own career is the mastery of a certain skill. This skill, whatever it may be, can be the keystone of your success.

Henry K.: A Question of Freedom

Henry K. worked for a large computer company as a marketing manager. As he approached his fifteenth year with the company, Henry was faced with a dilemma. If he accepted the promotion he knew he was about to be offered, he would receive a substantial pay increase and a very attractive retirement package—a situation some refer to as the golden handcuffs. Although many would feel fortunate to be in this position, Henry was troubled. He liked managing people and marketing computers, but he didn't like being "a small fish in a big pond" or having to deal with the personalities of his superiors. He also didn't like the complex process required for making changes in his operation. In short, he wanted to be more the master of his own fate than he could be in a large corporation.

After some careful assessment of his skills and some elaborate business planning, Henry decided to say no to the golden handcuffs and use his formidable marketing skills in his own shop. He opened a personal computer store, developed some very innovative marketing programs, and is doing great business. The key to Henry's success, besides sound planning and courage, was the realization that it was his expertise in marketing, not his role in the company, that was the real ticket to his prosperity.

Denise J.: Finding Unique Needs and Filling Them

Denise J. worked for an executive search firm. Her specialty was finding upper-level managers to fill unique needs in her client companies. She had an uncanny ability to find the right people for the right positions. She was highly respected and well paid, but she wasn't really interested in the kind of personnel placement she spent her time doing. Her real love was interior design, as she realized when she found that she spent much of her time in client companies focusing on how they could make better use of their environments. Although she was no expert in design, she had a real feeling for the field. After some careful thinking, it occurred to her that there must be people who design offices and that they must need people to generate business for them. Through some networking, she got the names of several office design firms and approached them. Her big selling point was that she had experience creating matches between her company's clients and her client companies.

Denise eventually landed a job as an account manager with a large design firm. She spends most of her time marketing her company's services but takes a unique slant. She carefully studies the design needs of the client and then suggests the designer from her group whose skills are best suited to that particular job. Client companies feel they are getting customized attention—and they are—and designers get to work on projects that they find really appealing. Denise gets to continue using the matchmaking talents she used in the search firm, but now she is using them in an area that truly excites her.

Marion S.: A Penchant for Creating Teams

Marion was the president of a small community college and believed strongly in the team approach to organizational management. Each month, she would hold meetings with the entire college community—faculty, staff, and students— at which people were encouraged to bring up issues of concern. Each time a substantive issue surfaced, Marion would listen carefully and then create a team to work on the problem. Each team would consist of people who were most affected by and could have the greatest potential impact on the problem. Most often, the problems would be resolved by the next monthly meeting.

In addition, Marion would often form teams of employees to focus on other issues of concern. And although some people felt there were too many teams floating around the organization, no one could deny that problems got resolved quickly and effectively.

After seven years of effective team management, Marion lost her job as a result of a reorganization of the community college system. She tried to get another presidency, but after about six months of searching, she decided to pursue other directions. When she assessed her skills, she realized that the strongest thing she had going for her, other than her knowledge of educational systems, was her ability to build teams. Her search was taking place at a time when participatory management was gaining in popularity.

Marion decided that since she couldn't find work in education at the level she wanted, she would try another arena. She
developed a résumé that highlighted her team-building skills
and approached potential employers as an expert in participatory management. Eventually, she landed a job with a
consulting firm that specialized in innovative approaches to
management. She is now one of their two team-building
experts and is called in when a client company wishes to
enhance its teamwork.

Marion's case is a good example of someone who is unable to find work in their chosen field and decides instead to
rely on their skills. In fact, each of the people just discussed—
Henry, Denise, and Marion—found their success, not in the
depth of their knowledge, but in the strength of the primary
skills they had mastered.

Developing Mastery

The key to career mobility is skill mastery. First, you need to
develop a primary skill, such as Henry's ability to market,
Denise's ability to create matches, or Marion's ability to build
teams. Next, you need to develop skills that support your
primary one. When you've mastered your strongest area,
you should focus on developing complementary skills that
make you stand out from the rest of the crowd.

Yes, But Can You Balance a Chandelier on Your Forehead?

I recently witnessed one of the best examples of skill mastery
and the use of subsidiary skills I've ever seen. It was part of a
performance by the Shanghai Acrobats, a group from the
People's Republic of China. All the acts were quite remarkable: A man doubled over into a barrel fifteen inches in di-
ameter and came out the other end; three women balanced
their weight on each other's heads while balancing on the

rim of a bicycle; a team juggled fifteen-foot batons as though they were drumsticks. But there was one act that stood out for me because of its developmental nature and its illustration of skill mastery.

The acrobat began by balancing an egg on a stick on his forehead, then moved up to two eggs, then three, one on top of the other. Next he appeared with a wine glass balanced on his forehead. He proceeded to add layer upon layer of full wine glasses until the structure balanced on his head resembled an elaborate chandelier—complete with a dozen lit kerosene lamps—four layers high. As if that were not enough, he proceeded to play a quite melodic tune on the clarinet. To cap his performance, he ran—yes, ran—up two freestanding ladders. After dismantling the last bit of his glass sculpture without spilling a drop, he toasted the audience with the final glass of wine.

As I walked away from this performance, I couldn't help thinking how we limit ourselves by our perception of our abilities. The members of the troupe serve as a poignant metaphor of what is possible through commitment to the attainment of mastery. To become a member of the Shanghai Acrobats, you begin practicing at the age of six or seven. After about five years, you audition for a role in the troupe; and if accepted, you remain with the troupe for life. When you are too old to perform, you will stay on to teach the young your very special talents.

One lesson to be learned from these people is the value of expanding one's range of skills. Take the chandelier balancer. Most of the audience would have been quite taken with his balancing; he need not have played the clarinet or climbed the ladders. He chose to develop subsidiary skills that by themselves were not so spectacular but when combined with his primary balancing technique gave him a combination of talents unique in all the world. His approach also provided him some versatility. Should he cease to be able to balance proficiently, he can always perform the musical accompaniment for the troupe or join the tumblers or trapeze artists. In other words, he has many talents to offer.

The best path to freedom in your career is to master one skill thoroughly and then expand your range of capabilities by developing other compatible, supporting, yet diversified skills.

The Seven Sides of Every Organization

It used to be true that skill mastery was all you needed to be successful in your career. Unfortunately, the complexity brought on by the maturing of the industrial age and the beginning of the information age presents a host of variables that affect your career. Understanding organizational dynamics, although not necessarily critical to performing your work, has become essential to maintaining your career. In order to effectively manage your career and stay on top, you need to pay close attention to the politics, uses of power, structure, patterns of communication, history, agenda, and image of your organization.

Politics

Failure to pay attention to politics can be disastrous. Take the much-publicized case of Steve Jobs and Apple Computer. Many people wonder how Jobs, by many accounts the creative force behind Apple, managed to get himself ousted as head of the company. There are many differing accounts of the battle between Jobs and John Scully that led to the ending of Jobs' relationship with his brainchild. But one thing is certain: For all his genius, Steve Jobs lacked the political acumen, or perhaps the commitment to understanding organizational politics, that could have saved his role in his company. Had he taken the power of politics more seriously, perhaps he could have applied his formidable intelligence to the political challenges he faced and avoided what was undoubtedly one of the greatest losses of his career.

Although most people have less to lose than Jobs, the

consequences of political indifference can be just as devas-
tating. Understanding politics is not as overwhelming as it
may seem. Remember that everyone learns how to handle
politics early in life through interactions with family, friends,
and schoolmates. What often clouds the ability to be politically astute has more to do with attitude than with ability.
Most people are able to handle politics (you're forced to
every day). However, some people don't like the *idea* of politics and shy away from it. I call this the *Pollyanna approach*.
The Pollyanna approach takes the position that if you ignore
the political side of things, it will go away. This is simply not
true. Avoiding a political perspective on your organization
does not make you immune to the political goings-on; it just
makes you a pawn in someone else's game plan rather than
the center of your own.

**The political process
is like the aging process:
Either treat it gracefully,
or you will spend your life in fear of it.**

Politics, like aging, is a fact of life. Some people accept the
aging process and appreciate the opportunities that accompany it; others resent it and do all they can to fight the inevitable. There are many ways to camouflage physical aging—
dress, cosmetics, and even surgery—but everyone's body
grows old. Those who feel good about who they are regardless of their age are unencumbered by their mortality. People
like Katharine Hepburn, George Burns, and Bette Davis show
little sign of slowing down. In fact, Hepburn is more elegant
than ever, Davis more ornery, and Burns more clever. None
has attempted to deny their aging; in fact, they use their age
to enhance their professional roles.

In a similar way, those who understand that human beings
are by nature political use that knowledge, adapt to their
environment, and accept the fact that increasingly complex
politics comes with increased success. Like the aging ac-

tors, those who understand politics draw on prior experience to better manage their current situation. They don't deny the vulnerability that politics (like aging) creates; they embrace the opportunity it affords.

At the other extreme of the political spectrum is what I call the *barracuda approach*. The barracudas are the people in your organization who thrive on politics for its own sake. They love to manipulate others to get their way, and they spend most of their time doing what they call "keeping their eye on the ball." Unless you are one of them, you probably agree that they are not to be trusted. The sad thing about these people is that they spend almost all their time engaged in politics at the expense of their—and often others'—real work. I want to be clear that by talking about appreciating politics, I am not advocating the breeding of barracudas.

At this point, you may be wondering about your choices, since neither the Pollyanna nor barracuda approach seems to be workable. There is an alternative: the *realistic approach*. The realistic approach to politics maintains that unlike the Pollyanna, a person needs to acknowledge the presence of politics. It also maintains that unlike the barracuda, a person needs to acknowledge the potential abuses of politics and the loss of trust that can accompany a manipulative approach. In other words, effective career management involves the careful study of the political side of any situation balanced with behavior that acknowledges, but does not exploit, the power of politics.

Power

One of the ways to develop a better understanding of, and realistic approach to, your organization's politics is to understand the concept of power. In my management classes, I spend a session discussing power. I start by having the students write a brief definition of the word *power*. I always get a wide range of responses. Here are some of the more common ones.

Power is influence.
Power is money.
Power is time.
Power is control.
Power is freedom.
Power is getting people to do what you want.

Obviously, power means different things to different people. Understanding the complexity of power and the different ways people gain and use it in organizations will help you to make decisions and manage relationships that enhance your career.

The Six Sources of Personal Power

**If you don't appreciate your own power,
no one else will.**

You may choose not to exercise your power; powerful people do that all the time. However, not being aware of the ways in which you can be powerful or, equally important, the ways others in your organization gain power, can cost you in many ways.

Role Power

The most obvious source of personal power comes from position or title. The way people both outside and inside your organization see your position will differ depending on what you are called.

Here is a simple illustration of how seriously people treat titles. A friend of mine frequently travels to Manhattan to socialize; she used to work there and still has many contacts. The other day, she was at a typical party, at which everyone was asking everyone else what they do for a living—a habit for which we Americans are notorious. She noticed an inordinate number of people describing themselves as entrepreneurs. Amused, she recalled a party a year earlier when everyone described themselves as consultants. She reflected on how the term *consultant* had been replaced by the more flamboyant *entrepreneur*. In fact, consultant had become synonymous with "being between jobs," whereas entrepreneur meant "furthering your own and others' wealth and prosperity through creative endeavor."

Just as words like "consultant" and "entrepreneur" take on meanings in the marketplace other than their literal ones, words used as titles in organizations reflect one's status and thus one's power. A few years ago, I interviewed Daniel Levinson, author of *Seasons of a Man's Life* and an expert on relationships at work. Early in our discussion, he questioned me on my title, which at the time was "coordinator." When he found out I was totally responsible for my program, he strongly advised that I have my title changed to more accurately reflect my status. It has since been changed to "manager." Although such a change may at first seem inconsequential, it can make a big difference in how you are seen both within and beyond your organization. So to make the most of role power, be sure your title portrays you in the strongest way possible.

Another aspect of role power has to do with your perceived and actual purpose within the organization. Your role may be reflected in your title and may also go beyond it. Letting others know what your role is without being obnoxious can enhance people's view of your contribution, thus enhancing your power.

Persuasion Power

Persuasion power is quite different from role power in that it is not associated with rank. Anyone with the right skills and knowledge of what it takes to influence people can wield persuasion power. A few years ago, I bought a new house. The previous owner heated the basement with coal, a practice I did not wish to continue. I was left with eight barrels of coal to get rid of and decided to give them away. I posted signs all over town announcing the availability of the eight free barrels, but to my surprise, I got no response. After several days of pondering my failed effort, I realized my problem was that the coal was free. People are suspicious of free offers; free-gift marketing ploys have ruined us forever. So I decided to try a new approach.

**If you can't give it away,
sell it.**

That's right, I put up a new sign offering the coal at a "great price": eighty dollars for the eight barrels. I got several calls and sold the coal in a couple of days.

Getting people to do what you want, even when it is to their benefit, is not always easy, but understanding the basic principles of influence can help a great deal. You need to be careful that your plans do not backfire (when it comes to influence, a little knowledge *is* a dangerous thing). But if you keep the following ten principles in mind, you will probably be able to get what you want from others.

Ten Principles of Persuasion

1. If you want something to be considered valuable, make people pay for it in some way.
2. Once you've gotten someone to do what you want, encourage them to keep doing it until they develop a pattern of behavior.
3. Once they've developed an acceptable pattern, encourage them to continue by focusing on what you like about the pattern.
4. Make new requests seem as similar as you can to past activities that were popular. People respond to familiarity much more than to novelty.

5. Get people involved in a project as early as possible. Involvement breeds cooperation.

6. If people are doing what you want them to do, make it public. Publicity also breeds cooperation.

7. Enlist other people to help your persuasive efforts. People like to feel like they're part of a group, not simply following a leader.

8. Be clear about what you want from people when you approach them. Fear of making mistakes often contributes to resistant behavior.

9. Make your requests seem reasonable. People prefer doing what seems normal to what seems odd or bizarre.

10. When suggesting something new, let others in on how you arrived at your decision. Carefully constructed plans are better received than impulses.

Follow these principles of persuasion, and you will find people much more willing to cooperate with, and be led by, you. It will help both your career and theirs.

Relationship Power

I'm sure you're all familiar with people in your organization who seem to develop relationships with others more easily than most. One of the things that drives these people, aside from a genuine enjoyment of others, is the knowledge that strong relationships help build strong careers. People who understand relationship power know that treating everyone in the organization as an equal creates a base of support that the fanciest title could not provide.

Psychologists call this approach to human relationships the principle of *unconditional positive regard* (UPR). That is, all people are worthy of respect and deserve to be treated in a dignified fashion. Although it was formulated as a guide for therapists in working with clients, particularly difficult ones, the UPR principle is a good frame of reference for anyone. It can be particularly helpful when you meet someone, as we all do, that you just don't like. Having to deal with someone you don't enjoy working with can be a tremendous barrier to productivity. If you can employ the UPR principle when it feels most difficult, you'll be surprised at the positive results.

Just as you all know people who are good at building and maintaining relationships with others, you probably also know people who treat all but a select few like garbage. Aside from being poor humanitarians, these people are missing out on a great opportunity to increase their personal career power.

By treating everyone well, you maximize the smooth flow of work toward the achievement of your objectives. When you choose to be particular about who you're kind to, you create tremendous barriers to the achievement of your goals. I'm not talking about offering token praise to people in a patronizing fashion. I'm talking about treating everyone in your organization with a reasonable degree of respect.

If you're not yet convinced of the empowering effect of treating people well, think for a moment about the people who most often get abused. There's a good chance it's not the managers, the engineers, or the vice presidents; it's the secretaries, the clerks, and the production people. They are often referred to as the *front-line people,* and for good reason; they receive the most flack from the most people. Yet because of their multipurpose roles, they also have the most information. Developing good relationships with people who have access to important information is not only good human sense; it's good business sense.

The real challenge in maintaining relationships that empower you is treating people well when things are not going your way. For example, when I first tried to market myself as a writer, I had a management proposal out at a time when management books were proliferating. After about fifteen submissions (and fifteen rejections), my agent regrettably informed me that she didn't think she could sell my book. A friend suggested I try a different agent. I felt that she had done a good job and knew her business. So rather than abandon the relationship, I sent her flowers and thanked her for her continued work on behalf of my book. Her own perseverance, and, I believe, my renewed faith in her abilities led her to submit the beleaguered proposal to a few more publishing houses. One of them liked my style enough to suggest that I submit a different proposal, one for a career book. Although I didn't sign with that house, my agent submitted the new proposal to other houses, and the result is this book. If I had listened to my friend and dumped my agent before she dumped me, I might never have written the second proposal, let alone sold it.

It's easy to treat people well when they give you what you want. The challenge is to treat them well when you're not getting what you want.

Knowledge Power

Knowledge power comes from having a genuine understanding of what your organization provides, be it a product or a service. Knowledge power means being an expert either in the broadest sense, knowing everything there is to know about your product or service, or in a narrower sense, knowing a given aspect of that product or service, such as marketing or production. Whatever the case, knowledge power is unique in that it is the only source of power that cannot be taken away from you. Ironically, it is also the only source of power that can limit your advancement if used alone.

People who have a strong base in knowledge power are very good at what they do; however, they often find themselves stuck in highly technical positions. They are so good at what they do that people with other bases of power use their power to keep them in that place.

The most common mistake people with knowledge power make is assuming their mastery of their field will protect them. Although knowledge power gives you some leverage, particularly if you're the only one with the knowledge, it does not ensure your success. If you are concerned with having a superior career, not just with doing a superior job, you need to realize that knowledge alone will further your work but may not tap your full potential.

Tony G.: The Limitations of Being an Expert

Tony G. worked for a large manufacturing firm that specialized in designing and producing systems for use by major utilities. He was involved in the development of a transporter used to carry radioactive materials within the confines of a nuclear power plant. He was an expert on robotics design and the properties of radioactive materials. In his lab, he developed a transport system that he felt was superior in design, easier to manufacture, and equally safe compared with the models his company was manufacturing. Confident that management would see the wisdom in his design, Tony presented his plan to his superiors.

A few weeks later Tony was informed that his proposal had not been accepted. When he asked why, the response was a simple "no." Believing he had no recourse, he returned to his lab and went back to refining the old and, in his opinion, inferior product.

Tony's rejection was a result of his isolationist approach and overdependence on his knowledge power. Although his idea may have been a good one, he was powerless to influence others in his direction. As a master technician and nothing but a master technician, he lacked the ability to create what he was most capable of creating and left his company with an inferior product. Had Tony developed a stronger relationship with his superiors, he might have been able to sway them or at least get them to explain their objections. Had he developed his influencing skills, he might have been able to change their minds or present his case more strongly to begin with, thereby increasing his chances of acceptance.

Instead, he was left scratching his technologically superior head, forced to comply with inferior instructions.

Commitment Power

Throughout this book, I've talked about the power of belief and the importance of creating a picture of what you want in your career as a strategy for achieving success. The same principles for getting what you want can be applied to keeping what you have.

This idea is not new. Virtually all the management literature written over the past ten years talks about the importance of having and maintaining a vision for the organization. The management literature addresses the issue from the perspective of the organization, and the meeting of its goals, but I would suggest that it is equally important in the management of individual careers.

Articulating a vision for an organization and keeping others committed to that vision are difficult tasks. If management of others is an integral part of your career, you need to work on fostering their commitment. But although commitment is important, blind commitment to performing the tasks required of you by the organization is not enough. You need to consider your own role in the organization as one that simultaneously meets the organization's goals and your own career development goals. Gaining a sense of clarity of your own purpose in relation to the purpose of the organization will enhance your performance—and your image as a valuable organizational member.

If you cannot find a personal vision that is in line with the goals of the organization, it may be time to think about moving on. If you are not committed to the overall good of the organization, you will not be able to function at a high level of productivity. Without this personal drive toward high performance, your career will not realize its full potential. Lack of commitment is demoralizing and debilitating. Commitment is a powerful motivator. Don't live without it.

Loyalty Power

When it comes to your career, loyalty means having people around you who see your success as their success. Generating loyalty from subordinates, peers, and superiors, is not an easy thing, but if you can accomplish it, your career will be greatly enhanced. Like creating a network of supporters for your job search, creating a network of support for your work can make the difference between appearing competent and valuable and appearing merely adequate and dispensable.

The best way to foster loyalty on the part of colleagues is to create what psychologists call a *win-win situation*. A win-win situation means that both parties involved believe they will benefit from their association. The more you can foster this belief with people at work, the more likely you'll develop loyalty and the power that accompanies it. The best way to destroy loyalty is to communicate to others that you see yourself in competition with them. Unless you are in direct competition with a colleague, a situation some organizations foster, it is better to make that colleague a supporter. The more supporters you can develop, the more power you will have over your work and your career.

Structure

Every organization has a structure. There are almost as many structural variations as there are organizations. Identifying the primary structure of an organization can give you clues on how best to navigate through that system and, more important, whether a particular system is one you can live with, let alone thrive in.

The classic organizational structure in this country is the bureaucracy, that complex web of institutional rituals that demands certain procedures be adhered to whether or not they serve the immediate or long-term goals of the organization. If you find yourself in or about to enter one of these organizations beware.

Bureaucracies are the dinosaurs of the information age.

Because information is the foundation for the contemporary American organization, there is no room for organizational systems that, by their very nature, slow down its flow. If you're serious about your career and find yourself working in a bureaucracy, there are two things you can do that will prevent that system from holding you back: leave it or change it.

There are other types of systems that can provide a good environment for the development and maintenance of your career. About twenty years ago, a man named Rensis Likert developed a theory about organizations that suggested that most fall into one of four types of systems. These systems range from the highly autocratic to the highly participatory. Many companies now use the Likert scale to determine which type of system is in place. Some organizations believe one type of system is better than another and use the data gathered from the Likert scale to help them implement it. Understanding what type of system you're in or about to enter can make the difference between spinning your wheels and getting what you want. Here is a brief summary of the four types.

System 1: There is a high level of control at the top. Techniques for motivating people include fear, punishment, and occasional rewards. Most of the communication occurs from the top down.

System 2: Decision making occurs at the top, but there is some delegating of responsibility. Techniques for motivating people involve rewards and potential punishment. Most of the communication is also from the top down.

System 3: Policy decisions are made at the top, and specific operational decisions are made at lower levels. Techniques for motivating people primarily involve rewards for work well done. Communication tends to be more of a two-way street.

System 4: Decision making is widely dispersed. People are motivated by their actual involvement in meeting the organization's goals. Communication occurs constantly in every direction possible.

Organizational Systems and Your Career

When I was doing my doctoral research, I thought it would be interesting to study how the different systems might affect the career development of the people in them. What I found was quite eye-opening. The type of organizational structure has a direct impact on the extent to which people get the career development they need.

If you're working in a system 1 organization, opportunities for professional growth and development are limited, unless you see yourself—and they see you—moving up the organizational ladder. The advantages of working in this type of organization are that they tend to promote people from within and to be very hierarchical, with a lot of rungs on their career ladders. If your goal is to keep doing what you've been doing with increased responsibility, you might do well in a system 1 organization. Just make sure that it's what you want and that the upper rungs of the ladder are not too crowded.

A system 2 organization is also pretty authoritarian and usually has an elaborate hierarchy with lots of rungs for the right people to climb. The best way to decide if this type of organization is right for you is to determine whether what they want you to do for them matches what you feel you do best and is what you want to do. Because this type of organization tends to be fairly rigid, trying to create change can often be an exercise in futility. If you do feel the organization is the right place for you, the rewards for good work can be quite substantial. A good match with a type 2 organization can provide a place for you to further develop your primary and subsidiary skills.

A system 3 organization differs substantially from the first two in that it is much more flexible and consequently offers a greater range of career development opportunities. People are encouraged to communicate with superiors, and they are challenged and encouraged to expand their repertoire of skills. Here you are more likely to find role models with diverse talents, people genuinely interested in expanding your range of abilities. You are also more likely to be recognized for your ideas as well as your bottom-line results.

Perhaps the richest structure in terms of career development is the system 4 organization. In this type of system, people are encouraged to develop to their full potential in as broad a range of areas as possible; consequently, opportunities for career development are unlimited. This system is good for people who have a high ability to tolerate ambiguity. You never know what's coming down the pike next in a system 4 organization, and that's the way they like it. So if order and stability are important to you, stay away from these organizations. If you can handle ambiguity and can find a system 4 organization, grab onto it and hang on. The ride will be rocky but well worth it.

Leonard T.: What You See May Not Be What You Get

Leonard T. worked as a foreman for a large family business. Though not a member of the family, he was still able to move gradually up the organizational ladder. However, like many family businesses, this one was a system 1 organization. After ten years with the company, Leonard was shocked when he was passed over for a promotion in favor of a distant cousin of the owner.

After leaving the company, Leonard decided to find a less rigid employer, one that would help him to diversify his talents. He was offered a position in a manufacturing firm that claimed to be using a highly participative management approach, what we've been calling a system 4 organization. Leonard was very excited when he heard about the benefits this company offered, including unlimited sick time, rewards for high performance, and membership in problem-solving teams. After a few months, he discovered what the company was really like. Although there was unlimited sick time, you had to bring a note from your doctor if you were out. Rewards for high performance involved competing with your peers for who produced the most widgets. The worst part for Leonard was that if he was out sick, his problem-solving team partners were responsible for doing his work, which caused incredible feelings of resentment.

Leonard realized he had stumbled into an organization that was worse for his development than the system 1 organization he had left. He had landed in another, even more rigid, system 1 organization camouflaged as a system 4.

The most important thing to be learned from Leonard's experience is to take a careful look at the organization you're in or are thinking about joining. Examine its structure and determine how it will help your career development. Knowing where to go, what is there for you, and when to move on are key considerations for staying on top. Assessing the extent to which an organization's structure supports your career goals can be critical to your success.

Patterns of Organizational Communication

Understanding the patterns of communication within an organization is essential to operating effectively there. These patterns will influence your ability to get what you want, your productivity, and your strategies for staying on top. Understanding patterns of communication includes paying attention to the level of formality present in an organization, the norms of the organization, the extent to which people listen to one another, the impact of size on communication within the organization, and the flow of information.

Formality

Some organizations are very formal; others are less so. One way to assess the extent of formality is to focus on the amount of paper that gets passed around. Highly formal organizations usually have an abundance of paper work; highly informal organizations have almost none. You may not think this is particularly important in relation to your career, but it is. One of the key variables affecting promotion decisions is assessment of performance. If you're in a highly formal organization, there's a good chance you will participate in at least one performance review a year, with an elaborate report on your performance that would undoubtedly be used in promotion decisions. If this is the case, all you have to worry about is that your performance reviews reflect your accomplishments in the most positive light possible.

A highly informal organization with no formal performance reviews, let alone elaborate reports, presents a totally different scenario. More often than not, the assessment of your performance exists primarily in the minds of your superiors. Considering the frequency with which organizations change hands these days, relying on the informal, word-of-mouth appraisal can be dangerous. If you find yourself in one of these highly informal situations, you may choose to go along with the dominant culture and operate that way in your work. But when it comes to documenting your own performance, use every opportunity possible to get it and put it in writing.

Norms

If you look closely, you'll find that the organization in which you work has behavioral norms for communication. These norms tell you what the boundaries of communication are: who talks to whom about what. In some organizations, people talk freely about their work, the world, and their personal lives. In others, communication centers on solving work-related problems and nothing else. In some organizations, people cross hierarchical lines freely, communicating with peers, superiors, and subordinates; in others, people interact only within their level of the hierarchy. In other organizations, people cross lines in certain areas but not in others. Understanding the subtleties around the norms of communication in any organization can make the difference between being a strong communicator and someone to be trusted and being someone who intrudes on other peoples' personal space by violating the norms.

Listening

Perhaps the most talked about aspect of organizational communication is listening. If you are lucky, you have one or two people in your organization who really listen to you. Really listening means paying attention to what the other is saying, showing you understand, and *then* responding. Most people skip the understanding part and move right to responding. Instead of listening during communication, they spend their time thinking about what they're going to say when it's their turn to speak.

If you want to enhance your role in your organization and strengthen your position, stop second-guessing what others are saying and formulating your responses prematurely. If you want to develop strong relationships and expand what you already know, slow down your communication output and begin really listening to others. Do this, and you'll find people will tell you more about more important things, and you'll soon develop a reputation as someone the organization could not survive without.

Size

At first glance, it may appear that size and communication have nothing to do with each other, but this appearance is false. The larger the organization, the more complex the channels of communication, and the more difficult clear communication becomes. A friend of mine, who recently moved from a large university to a small community college, said it best: "In the past, if I had a problem, there was a building I had to go to to find the answer; now there's a person." This does not mean that smaller is always better, only that the difficulty associated with effective communication changes with size. In a large organization, it is more difficult to be heard and make an impact, but there are various channels available for communicating important ideas. Small organizations have more distinct channels of communication, but they pose other problems. If there is only one person in an area to receive your communication and that person is uninterested or unavailable, you may be left with no recourse.

Although the elaborate maze established by most large organizations can prove frustrating, the possibility that there are multiple recipients of your message makes some communication possible and your desires in relation to that communication more attainable.

It is also important to make sure the message you are communicating is presented in a way that is easily understood by your audience. Communicating in the most palatable way possible is important regardless of the size of your organization. Pay attention to the way size affects the channels of communication. Understanding what is acceptable and what is not, in the context of a given system, can make the difference between being heard and being lost in the crowd. Careful attention to both form and content will enhance your message and your performance as a communicator.

Flow of Information

I talked earlier about how people are bombarded with so much information that most of it does not get processed. Becoming a master communicator requires becoming an

expert manager of the flow of information. To further understand this concept, consider the computer as a metaphor.
Imagine that you are the computer and that your ability to
manage the flow of information is represented by the software. Anyone who's worked with a computer knows that it is
only as good as its software. A good software program is one
that has plenty of information, organizes it in an efficient
manner, and knows when and how to present it to the user.
Many software programs don't make it because they give
the user too much information at the wrong time. The good
programs are organized so that the only information presented is what is needed and usable at the time. The really
good programs also make information retrieval easy.

Similarly, a master communicator understands the flow of
information in a particular environment. He or she appreciates the various modes for delivering information—one-to-
one conversation, meetings, memos, phone calls, reports,
and so on—and carefully weighs the information, the
receiver's receptivity, the timing, and the context before deciding when and how to send the communication. The master communicator realizes the importance of acceptance and
appreciates the role the sender plays in that acceptance before sending the message. Finally, the master communicator
realizes that when it comes to managing the flow of information, the medium—that is, the delivery—*is* often the message.

History

I asked a friend who is a historian what impact she thought
history played in the life of an organization and in the lives of
its members. She said simply, "Everything is history." What I
think she meant was that nothing exists in the present that
doesn't have a past. To understand the present, you must
understand the past. Therefore, if you are to manage a career in an organization, it makes sense that you need to
understand the organization's past. A knowledge of your

organization's origins and history can give you a unique perspective that will help you stay on top as you move within,
and perhaps beyond, that organization. Such things as when
the organization was founded, by whom, and for what purpose can provide valuable information on what makes it tick.
In addition, understanding the transitions an organization
has gone through before your time can sometimes save you
from making major mistakes. Although the saying "history
repeats itself" may be true, you certainly want to avoid dupli-
cating the blunders of your predecessors.

Paying attention to recent history can keep you from making mistakes in the present. I recently worked with a client
who took a job with a young entrepreneurial company because he thought it would be a good place to gain some
management experience. He became manager of a manufacturing plant that was having production problems. After a
week on the job, he realized the plant's problems involved
more than the need to refine the production process. Apparently, the owner of the company believed the problem was
one of motivation while the production workers believed it
was one of outdated equipment. This new manager was the
third to be hired in a six-month period; the other two quit
after two months each because they were unable to bridge
the gap between management and workers. The new manager found himself in a no-win situation, unable to reconcile
either party to the other's position. Had he taken the time,
before accepting the position, to study the organization's
recent history, he could have set some conditions that would
have alleviated the problem. If he did not get the conditions
he asked for, he could have continued his search and found a
more manageable situation. Instead, he found himself stalemated and contemplating resignation.

Agenda

I use the word *agenda* to cover a variety of things, including
the goals, objectives, mission, and priorities of an organiza-

tion. Understanding an organization's agenda is critical to understanding what needs to be done. Many factors influence the agenda, ranging from a definition of the product or service to a philosophy of management to an attitude about people. Having a clear picture of the organization's agenda before joining it and tracking the agenda as it changes while you're there can make the difference between staying on top and hitting rock bottom.

A Question of Priorities

A couple of years ago, I went to visit a friend who worked in Human Resource Development at one of the large computer companies. Because her office was in corporate headquarters, I asked her for a tour. She obliged and introduced me to the various human resource people in the different divisions.

The HRD people in research and development were located in the penthouse. Their space was quite impressive, down to the oak in and out boxes. The HRD folks in marketing were halfway down the tower. They were a very enthusiastic group with ample space, and I was impressed with their frenetic pace and overflowing plastic in and out boxes. Finally, we visited the HRD people in manufacturing, who were in a bit of disarray, having just moved their office for the third time in eight months. I couldn't spot an in or out box anywhere.

During lunch with my friend, I said, "It seems to me that your company's top priority is developing new products. They also seem terribly concerned with getting their products to market. However, I was surprised at their lack of commitment to manufacturing."

She looked at me and said, "That's very accurate. Where'd you get that information?"

I replied, "I saw it in your in and out boxes."

The key to understanding an organization's agenda is to keep your eyes and ears open. Had I decided to join her company, as I later learned she had intended, I would have found very different work depending on which HRD door I entered—research and development, marketing, or manufacturing. The point is: If you are to stay on top in your career, you need to pay attention to the priorities and the way those priorities change within and around your organization. You must be keenly aware of the implications of those changes on your own career. For example, about two months after my visit, the executive in charge of all the company's HRD units resigned. All HRD staff now report to personnel; the leaders of the various divisions are in shock, and many have already resigned. Had I accepted what looked like a very attractive offer two months earlier, I would have been on the street with them or, worse, treading water.

Many a competent captain has gone down with a sinking ship.

Paying attention to the agenda and shifting priorities of an organization can tell you when to stay put and when to consider a move. If you watch the signals, both subtle and overt, carefully, you can do a lot to ensure you stay on top.

Image

Every organization projects an image. The best way to understand image is to look at high-profile organizations that work to project a certain image in order to sell their products. In fact, image has become so powerful as a marketing device that it often has nothing to do with the product, the service, or the organization. Consider for a moment the case of Pepsi Cola and singer Michael Jackson. Pepsi reportedly has spent millions of dollars employing Jackson for TV commercials, the rationale being that the mere association of his image with the company will sell more soda pop.

Popular music of the 1960s is now being widely used by merchandisers to sell everything from running shoes to high-priced automobiles. It's no coincidence that the image these merchants are trying to create is one that the children of the 1960s (who are the consumers of the 1980s) find most attractive. Yet it would be a grave mistake to assume that working in one of these organizations would evoke the same nostalgic feelings. An organization's projected image and its day-to-day reality are quite often two very different things.

Just as companies project a certain image to the public to market their products, many organizations project a certain image to the work force to attract the best people. Staying on top when moving from one organization to another requires an ability to identify the image an organization is trying to project and the extent to which that image is an accurate reflection of what really goes on.

Image can be projected in a variety of ways. In the case of large, high-profile organizations, the media are a primary source of image building. Smaller organizations with fewer resources have other ways of promoting themselves.

There are several new service chains emerging in this country dedicated to creating good images for small businesses. This trend reflects the importance of image and the increasingly difficult task of cutting through the image-making machinery. The more important image becomes, the more resourceful the image makers get, and the more difficult it becomes to separate appearance from substance. It is conceivable, for example, that you could employ a medium-sized firm from another part of the country to do some work for you (perhaps real estate or investing) only to find that the firm consists of one person. Absurd as this may sound, many investors have lost large sums of money putting their faith in organizations whose only true asset was a superior but totally false image.

When considering a change within or beyond your organization, be sure the image you're getting is an accurate projection of what that organization is really like.

Mergers, Buyouts, Acquisitions, and Your Career

**The next time you find yourself
sitting on top of the world, enjoy it;
but remember, the world turns.**

It is fitting that this book should end with a discussion of the greatest challenge to managing your career: the increasing volatility of the marketplace and the resulting lack of predictability of the organizations in which you work. Throughout this book, I've talked about the changing nature of career stability in this country and the need to be at the center of your own career management rather than relying on the organization to take care of you. This does not mean the organization does not play a crucial role in your success. Careful attention to the ways an organization is changing during a transition can make the difference between landing on your feet and falling flat on your face.

**Ask not what your company
can do for you;
ask what you can do for your company.**

If you find yourself swept up in a major transition—a merger, buyout, or acquisition—and you've been a loyal employee for many years, don't make the mistake of thinking that your loyalty will protect you. Your best chance for survival is to present your potential value to the new organization, not to try and claim your right to remain because of past accomplishments. Many people who find themselves in a chaotic transition hope and often expect that their carefully developed track record will carry them through. The problem is, particularly in the case of mergers, that you are suddenly competing with people in the parent organization, some of whom are armed with equally impressive track records. As with any competitive situation, your past successes will not assure present success. Your past accomplishments can support your case, but your current performance and your potential to deliver in the future are the most important factors in surviving this kind of transition.

Another disconcerting but real possibility is that the new management may not appreciate your loyalty to the old management. This is particularly true if the takeover battle was a bloody one, as they often are. Although it is sometimes difficult to shift your approach, appearing loyal to the old guard and selling yourself based on your loyal performance will only serve to alienate rather than endear you to the new guard. Be prepared to present your past as a means for supporting your potential for future performance, but most important, show them what you can do for them.

EPILOGUE

CareerMap Itinerary

I've covered a lot of ground with you in nine chapters. Charting your own future by its nature encompasses a vast territory. I offer this final brief summary of key concepts to leave you with a frame for your travels.

- Maintain a set of empowering beliefs that fosters the attainment of your goals.
- Shift negative beliefs to positive beliefs so that they don't limit your efforts.
- Develop a clear view of yourself through assessment of:
  - your personal priorities
  - your work style
  - your interests, skills, and knowledge areas
  - your preferred culture
  - your vision of your own success
- Cultivate a rich pool of options from which to consider making changes.
- Use other people to help expand the possibilities.
- Be aware of the forces that prevent you from acting or changing, and develop strategies to combat them.
- Develop strategies for taking risks that maximize your possibilities but ensure your safety.
- Refine your job search strategies through:

- Persuasive paper work
- Occupational investigation
- Influential interviewing
- Networking
- Tracking leads
- Fine-tune your negotiation skills to always get the best deal possible.
- Build a base of relationships with people in your sphere of influence.
- Develop a power base for staying on top.
- Refine your organizational-diagnosis skills so that you will be better equipped to know what to do and when to do it.
- Finally, have a good time. Your career should be a wellspring of opportunity, not a burden.

I wish you success in creating your own CareerMap and charting your own future!

Dr. Neil Yeager presents lectures and seminars and consults in a variety of areas, including career management, organization development, risk taking, managing change, mentoring, and leadership. For more information, call or write:

Neil Yeager
P.O. Box 207
Hadley, MA 01035
(413) 545-1957

INDEX

Advocating, 211–213
American Dream, The, 60
Apple Computer, 231

Baryshnikov, Mikhail, 194
Beliefs, 8–13, 241
Blanchard, Ken, 89
Blowing your own horn, 79–81
Bolles, Richard, 140
Boston Celtics, 51
Bureaucracies, 243
Burns, George, 232

Career
    climbing path, 180
    expansive path, 180–181
    ladders, 181
    mobility, 229
    paths, 179–182
    stable path, 179–182
    visualization. See Visualization
CareerMap Profile, 13,16,18–55
    sample of options for, 64
Change, 84, 95–96
    and ability to function, 84–86
    and alternatives within organiza-
        tions, 88–89
    in career, 59
    demons and disciples of, 74–95
    excuses for avoiding, 74–95
    and getting started, 86–88
    inevitability of, vi, 74
    in job design, 88–89
    in the marketplace, 74–75
    wanting to, 95–96
Cheers, 139
Cialdini, Robert, 207

Coaching, 194–196
Coleco, 16–17
Commitment power, 193, 241
Communication, patterns of or-
        ganizational, 247–250
Company loyalty, 190
Competencies, 35
CORE Group, 61–69
    formation guidelines for, 62–63
Corporate patriarchy, 191
Cousins, Norman, 214
Cover letters, 131–133
Cross-gender relationships,
        217–218
Crystal, John, 140
Cuban Missile Crisis, 199
Culture, 48–50
    casing the organizational,
        171–175
    interviewing and, 173–175
    and job matching, 170–171
    organizational artifacts of, 172
    organizational rituals and, 177
    personal culture cluster, 50
    and the physical environment,
        171–172
    six sources of information on,
        175–177

Davis, Bette, 232
DECWORLD, 137
Department of Labor, Bureau of
        Labor Statistics, 48, 149
Dersu Uzala, 192–193
Digital Equipment Corporation,
        137
Dyslexia, 10

Edison, Thomas, 10
Einstein, Albert, 10
Emperor Jones, The, 93–94
Empowerment, 193, 238
Entrepreneurs, 234–235

Fantasies. *See* Visualization
Fear, 91–94
Fired, getting, 93–94
Fortune magazine, 59
Fosse, Bob, 194
Fowler, Mary Louise, 196
Friendship, 215–216

Goals, 75–76, 241
   individual vs. organizational,
      90–91
   and relationships, 237–238
Guthrie, Woody, 224

Hamblett, Theora, 142–143
Hart, Gary, 99
Having it all, 58–59
Helping. *See* Nondirective helping
Hepburn, Katharine, 232
Herman, Pee Wee, 139
History, 250
   and organizational positions,
      178
Homer, 191
How to Get Pregnant, 86

Iacocca, Lee, 170
Image, 172, 241, 253–254
Imagery, 51
Influence, 147, 207–209
Information, 153–155, 249
   as currency, 136–137
   gathering of, 138–143
   and relationships, 238–239
   sorting of, 85, 249–250
Information age, v, 136–137, 139,
      205, 231, 243
Inspiration, 213–214
Interests, 2, 33
Interviewing, 143–153
   and being yourself, 152–153
   group, 146

informational, 140–141
   and persuasion, 147–149
   and poor performance, 79–80
   stories and, 147–149
   stress, 145
   and style, 149–152
   style reference key, 151–152
   style screen, 150
   ten tips for better, 144–147
Intuition, 142–143, 159, 173, 187

Jackson, Michael, 253
Job market
   changes in, vi
   The Compelling, 137–143
   hidden, 137–138
Job satisfaction, 20, 24
Jobs, Steve, 231

Kennedy, John F., 199
Kennedy, Ted, Jr., 9
Kissinger, Henry, 81
Knowledge, 2, 35, 41
   power, 239–241
   scan, 39–41
Kolb, David, 30

Laziness, 92–94
Lead tracking pattern, 163
Learning styles, 30
Letters, 130–137
   of approach, 133–136
   art of writing, 130–131
   cover, 131
   and gatekeepers, 136
   how to write, 131–132, 135
   rejection, 12
   samples of, 132–133, 135–136
   thank you, 136
Levinson, Daniel, 192, 235
Levinson, Harry, 190
Likert, Rensis, 243
Likert scale, 243
Listening, 139–140, 148, 248
Lovesick, 84
Loyalty, 193, 255
   power, 193, 242
Luck, 82-84, 87

Mandala, The Great, 220
Massachusetts, University of, 83
Mentor, 191
Mentoring, 191–221
   cross-gender, 217–218
   multiple relationship, 218–221
   performance mentoring activi-
     ties, 193–204
   personal mentoring activities,
     204–216
Mergers, buyouts, and acquisi-
     tions, 90–91, 190–191,
     255–256
Midas touch, 141–142
Midlife crisis, 95
Mismanagement in the Human
     Service Agency, 199
Mission, 251–252
Mississippi, University of, 142–143
Modeling, 162–166, 198–201
   profile on heroic, 200–201
   tracking model profile, 165–166
Modesty, 80

Naisbitt, John, 138
National Institute of Mental Health,
   51
Negotiation, 182–187
   and changing careers, 185–186
   and getting a raise, 185
   and government jobs, 185
   six myths and realities of salary,
     183–187
Networking, 153–159
   computers and, 153–154
   exposure through, 157–159
   formal angles for, 155–156
   informal angles for, 156–159
   use of contacts in, 13
Newsweek magazine, 224
Nondirective helping, 201–204
   on being a nondirective helper,
     204
Norms. *See* Organizations
Nose for news, 141

Occupational investigation,
   136–143

Old-boy network, 192
Old dogs, 78–79
O'Neill, Eugene, 93
Opportunity
   lack of, 75–77
Options, 19, 58–69
   abundance of, 58
   generating of, 61–63
   sorting of, 65–69
Organizations
   agenda of, 251–252
   and commitment, 193
   communication patterns in,
     247–250
   image of, 172, 253–254
   juggling dynamics of, 212–213
   models of, 218–220
   norms and, 216
   participatory, 243, 246
   seven sides of, 231–254
   structure of, 242–246
   systems and your career,
     243–246

Paperwork, persuasive, 116–136
   creating your own, 117–118
Pepsi Cola, 253
Personal culture cluster, 50
Persuasion, Ten Principles of,
     236–237
POINT Process, The, 116–165
Politics, 81–82, 231–233
   barracuda approach to, 233
   Pollyanna approach to, 232
   realistic approach to, 233
Positions, health and stability of,
     177–178
Power, 233–242
   six sources of personal, 234–242
Preferred work style, 23–33
   assessment questionnaire, 24–29
   and interviews, 149–152
   in managing relationships, 30
   in organizational life, 32
   style explanation chart, 31
Priorities, 2, 20
   blocks, 21
   planning, 23

realignment of, 60–61
shift in, 20
Profile. *See* CareerMap Profile
Promoting, 205–209
  word of mouth, 207–208
Promotion Principle, The, 206

Quality of work life, 215

Reframing, 8–13
Relationship power, 237–239
Résumés, 116–130
  descriptive paragraphs for,
    123–127
  how to write, 118–120
  and personal style, 130
  samples of, 120–123
  ten tips for better, 127–130
Risk assessment process,
    104–112
Risk taking, 12, 98–113
  action plan for, 111–112
  and ambiguity, 102–104
  and the fear of loss, 106–108
  and friendship, 215
  mastering, 100–102
  Renaissance, 102–104
  structured and fluid nature of,
    112–113
Robbins, Anthony, 213
Rogers, Carl, 201
Role power, 234–235
Rush, Jennifer, 163–164
Russell, Bill, 51

Salary negotiation. *See* Negotia-
    tion
Scully, John, 231
Security, 190
Serendipity, 82–84
Service society, 137, 153
Shanghai Acrobats, 229–231
Showcasing, 209–211
Siegel, Dr. Bernie, 51
Significant events review, 36

Sixth sense, 142
Skill mastery, 226–231
Skills, 2, 35–47
  inventory, 41–47
  in marketing, 226–227
  in matching needs, 227–228
  in team management, 228–229
Springsteen, Bruce, 137, 224–225
Staying on top, guidelines for,
    225–226
Stock market, 17, 110
Stretching, 196–198
Support groups, 62

Taking risks. *See* Risk taking
Talking Heads, 216
Teams, creating, 228–229
Telemachus, 191
Time magazine, 224
Time, management of, 89
Toastmasters, 20
Tracking leads, 159–166
  through effective patterning,
    161–166
  finding models for, 164–166
Trust, 215

Ulysses, 191
Unconditional positive regard,
    237–238

Vision, 143, 241
Visualization, 50–54
  work visualization analysis, 53
  work visualization exercise,
    52–54

Wilson, Woodrow, 10
Workplace culture. *See* Culture

Yeats, William Butler, 10

Zero Advancement Principle, The,
    179–181